The Theory Of Credit, Volume 2, Issue 1...

Henry Dunning Macleod

THEORY OF CREDIT

εἰ δέ τοῦτο ἀγνοεῖς ὅτι Πίστις Ἀφορμὴ τῶν πασῶν ἐστι μεγίστη
πρὸς χρηματισμον, πᾶν ἂν ἀγνοήσειας

If you were ignorant of this that **Credit** is the greatest
Capital of all towards the acquisition of Wealth, you would
be utterly ignorant

DEMOSTHENES

Credit has done more, a thousand times, to enrich nations
than all the mines of all the world

DANIEL WEBSTER

THE
THEORY
OF
CREDIT

BY

HENRY DUNNING MACLEOD, M.A.

OF TRINITY COLLEGE, CAMBRIDGE, AND THE INNER TEMPLE, BARRISTER-AT-LAW

SELECTED BY THE ROYAL COMMISSIONERS FOR THE DIGEST OF THE LAW TO PREPARE
THE DIGEST OF THE LAW OF BILLS, NOTES, ETC.

HONORARY MEMBER OF THE JURIDICAL SOCIETY OF PALERMO, AND OF THE SICILIAN
SOCIETY OF POLITICAL ECONOMY;

CORRESPONDING MEMBER OF THE SOCIÉTÉ D'ÉCONOMIE POLITIQUE OF PARIS, AND OF
THE ROYAL ACADEMY OF JURISPRUDENCE AND LEGISLATION OF MADRID

IN TWO VOLUMES

VOLUME II.—PART I

LONDON:

LONGMANS, GREEN AND CO.

AND NEW YORK: 15, EAST 16TH STREET

1890

WORKS IN ECONOMICS

By the AUTHOR

Elements of Political Economy. 1858

A Dictionary of Political Economy. Vol. I. 1862

The Principles of Economical Philosophy. Two Vols. 1872-75

Lectures on Credit and Banking. 1882

*** *The above Works are out of Print*

42720

The Theory and Practice of Banking. Two Vols. Fourth Edition.
1836-86. Vol. 1. Price 12/- Vol. II. Price 14/-

The Elements of Economics. 2 Vols. 1881-86. Price 7/6 each Vol.

The Elements of Banking. 1 Vol. Ninth Edition. Price 5/-

Economics for Beginners. 1 Vol. Fourth Edition. Price 2/6

Theory of Credit. 2 Vols.
Vol. II., Part II. in the Press.

PREFACE

I HAVE deemed it expedient to publish Part I of Volume II at once, as its subject may be of interest in the immediate future

Volume I contains the complete exposition of the Fundamental Conceptions and the great Scientific and Juridical Principles of Credit

The Part now published exhibits the practical application of these Principles in the business of Commerce—in the mechanism of Banking, in which it will be seen how erroneous the popular notions on the subject are—and the Foreign Exchanges.

In this exposition of the actual mechanism of the colossal System of Credit will be seen the verification of Daniel Webster's aphorism—" **Credit has done more, a thousand times, to enrich nations than all the mines of all the world** "

In Chapter IX, I have pointed out the fallacy of the opinions of Mill and many others, on the nature of the Funds, or Public Credit

Chapter X contains an examination of the influence of Money and Credit on Prices and the Rate of Interest, upon which, at their request, I laid an elaborate Paper before the late Gold and Silver Commission

LONDON:

A. P. BLUNDELL, TAYLOR & Co., Printers, 177, Upper Thames Street. E.C.

CONTENTS

OF

THE SECOND VOLUME

PART I

CHAPTER VI

ON COMMERCIAL CREDIT

CHAPTER VII

THE THEORY OF BANKING

CHAPTER VIII

ON THE FOREIGN EXCHANGES

CHAPTER IX

ON THE NATURE OF THE FUNDS

CHAPTER X

ON THE INFLUENCE OF MONEY AND CREDIT ON PRICES
AND THE RATE OF INTEREST

CREDIT

CHAPTER VI

ON COMMERCIAL CREDIT

1. Having investigated the complete Juridical and Mathematical Theory of Credit ; or the Creation, Transfer or Circulation and Extinction of the Goods, Chattels, Commodities, Merchandise, or Economic Quantities, termed Credits or Debts, we have now to exhibit its practical application in commerce, in the two following chapters. In this chapter we shall explain the mechanism of Commercial Credit : *i.e.*, where Credit is used to transfer or circulate existing commodities or to produce them

On **Credit** *created to* **Transfer** *or* **Circulate existing commodities**

2. Goods or commodities in the ordinary course of business pass through the following hands—

1. The grower, or foreign importer
2. The manufacturer
3. The wholesale dealer
4. The retail dealer
5. The customer or consumer

To the first four of these persons the goods are **Capital**: because they grow or import them, manufacture or deal in them, for the sake of profit.   The fifth buys or consumes them for the sake of profit.   The price the consumer pays for them must evidently be sufficient to reimburse the original expenses of production

Now, leaving out of consideration for the present how the foreign importer of the goods obtained them, which concerns the foreign trade of the country, and which we do not touch upon here— if he sells the goods for ready money to the wholesale dealer or manufacturer he can, of course, immediately import or produce a further supply of goods in the room of those he has disposed of.

In a similar way, the wholesale dealer sells to the retail dealer; and, if the retail dealer pays him in ready money, he might immediately effect further purchases from the merchant to supply the place of the goods he had sold

So if the retail dealer were always paid in ready money by the consumer he might replace the part of his stock that was sold

And so, if everybody had always ready money at command, the stream of production or circulation might go on uninterruptedly as fast as Consumption or Demand might allow. Thus the Circulation or Production, of which we have shown that Circulation is one form, would be effected by money, which would, in this case, be the Circulating Medium

But this is far from being the case.   Few or no persons have always ready money at command for all the purposes which they require.   Very few traders can commence with enough ready money to pay for all their purchases: and if the stream of Production or Circulation were to stop until the Consumers had paid for the goods in money, it would be vastly diminished

Now, if the wholesale dealer sees that there is a certain demand for goods, if he has no money, and the merchant will not sell the goods to him except for ready money—there will be no Circulation and no Profits

Now, as Mill says—"Wealth is *anything* which has purchasing power"

Suppose that the merchant has confidence in the wholesale dealer's character and integrity, he sells the goods to the wholesale dealer on Credit : that is, he sells him the goods, and, instead of the actual money, he takes his Promise to pay three months after date. That is, he sells the goods for a Credit, Debt, or Right of action, instead of for money

Now this case is a **Sale** exactly as if the goods were sold for Money. The merchant cedes the Property in the goods to the dealer, exactly the same in one case as in the other

Hence we see that Credit has caused exactly the same Circulation or Production as Money does. Hence Credit is Circulating Medium exactly as Money is

This Debt, or Right of action, so created, may be recorded in two ways—

1. As a simple Debt in the merchant's books
2. It may be recorded in a Bill of Exchange

But it is quite clear that the Property is exactly the same in whichever form it is : it has equally circulated commodities, and the claim as a Right of action is equally valid in one form as the other : though one form may have more conveniences than the other : and the Book Debt can at any time be transformed into a Bill of Exchange at the will of the parties

In a similar manner the wholesale dealer may sell the goods on Credit to the retail dealer, and the Credits, Debts or Rights of action, may be recorded in two different ways, either as Book Debts, or as Bills of Exchange. As in the former case the same Circulation or Production has been effected by Credit as by Money

Lastly, the retail dealer may sell the goods on Credit to the Consumer or Customer, and this Debt may also be recorded in two forms : either as a Book Debt or a Bill of Exchange. In this case, however, the Debt most usually rests as a simple Book Debt : it is very seldom in the form of a Bill of Exchange

Thus, we see that Credit has exactly the same effect in circulating goods through every stage as Money : hence Credit is Circulating Medium exactly as Money : and that all the Debts in the books of traders are part of the Circulating Medium of the country just as much as Bills of Exchange : which was the universal doctrine of statesmen until Lord Overstone perverted men's minds on the subject

Moreover, at each transfer, it is necessary to create a new Credit, Debt, or Right of action : thereby exemplifying the

B 2

distinction we have already pointed out between Credit and Bills of Lading : because if the goods had passed through so many transfers the same Bill of Lading would always have accompanied them

Now, the Credit, Debt, or Right of action for which the merchant sold the goods to the wholesale dealer is, no doubt, valuable Property to him, because he knows that it will be paid in due course. Similarly the Debts for which the other parties sold the goods are also Valuable Property to them. Credit, even so far as this, would greatly conduce to Production or Circulation : and the vast amount of it generated in this way would be valuable Property to its owners. But in this state it would be of no further use to them. It might, therefore, be aptly compared to so much dead stock : the next step is to convert it into so much living stock

Credits *made* Saleable

3. It appears from Sir Francis Child[1] that before the institution of Banks in this country commercial bills were not transferable : it was supposed that it was contrary to the Common Law

He says that it was the custom in Holland that every person who bought goods on Credit should give his note for the payment, which the seller of the goods could put into circulation like so much Money, and make use of in further purchases. He was very anxious that this practice should be introduced into England : but he says that the Common Law did not allow it : in which, however, he was mistaken

The next step, therefore, is to make this dead stock negotiable, or exchangeable, *i.e.*, to make the Debts themselves saleable commodities : to sell them in exchange for other goods like money : or to sell them for ready money : or for other Debts for more convenient amounts, and immediately exchangeable for Money on demand : and, therefore, equivalent to Money

The history of Bills of Exchange is so obscure in this country that we cannot tell when it arose ; but, in process of time, traders found that they could use the Bills which they took in exchange for their goods to purchase other goods with : and those persons

[1] *A Discourse on Trade*

who sold their goods for the Bills used them to purchase other goods with. Thus, it was found that Bills of Exchange could circulate in commerce and effect exchanges in exactly the same way as Money, until they were paid off and extinguished: being indorsed at every transfer for the sake of securing their payment. Thus Bills of Exchange became a great Circulating Power, or Medium. At one time the Circulating Medium of Lancashire consisted almost entirely of Bank of England Notes and Bills of Exchange, which sometimes had 150 indorsements on them before they became due

But there are two classes of traders whose especial business it is to buy these Commercial Debts, either for Money or for Credit immediately convertible into Money: and, therefore, equivalent to Money

The first class of these traders are called Bill Discounters, *i.e.*, buyers of Debts: they buy these Debts with actual Money

The second class are called **Bankers** : they buy commercial Debts by creating other Debts payable on demand

The sale of Commercial Debts seems to have been begun when the Goldsmiths became bankers. Having large sums deposited with them for which they agreed to pay heavy interest, and which were repayable on demand, they perceived that the most profitable way of trading was to discount Bills with their own Credit : and the Bills maturing at short intervals, brought their money back to them, so that they could always meet the claims upon them

Thus, all traders who received Bills in exchange for goods found a market where they could immediately convert their Bills payable at a future time into ready money

The mechanism of Banking will be exhibited in the next chapter

Upon Accommodation Bills

4. The bills which we have been considering arose out of past transactions. The merchant having sold his goods to the trader for a Right of action, he may sell this Debt to his banker. If the banker discounts the bill he has two names as securities, first the acceptor of the bill or the buyer of the goods, who is the Debtor primarily responsible, or principal debtor as he is called : and, secondly, his own customer who indorses the bill to him, and so becomes security that if the principal debtor does not pay the bill he will

But banking credits may be created to effect future transactions as well as to buy the debts created by past transactions

Suppose that a merchant wishes to effect a purchase, he may request his banker to discount his Promissory Note so as to obtain a Credit to effect his purchase.   But the banker will not improbably say to him that it is against his rules to discount any instrument containing only one name : but, that, if he can get any responsible friend to stand security for him, by indorsing his Note, that he will discount it for him.   Suppose, then, that some responsible friend agrees to be security for him, and without having received any consideration indorses the Note : such an instrument would be an **Accommodation Note**

And, when any person puts his name on a bill to stand security for its payment, without having received any consideration for doing so ; it is termed an **Accommodation Bill**

The banker now having, say, two names on the instrument, discounts it : and the merchant, having now a Credit at his account, purchases goods, the proceeds from the sale of which are intended to meet the bill when it is due

Now, it is evident that the security of this bill, which is an Accommodation Bill, is exactly the same as if it had been a real bill

What difference can it make whether a bill which arose out of a *past* transaction is sold for a banking credit, or a bill is sold for a banking credit which is immediately applied to purchase goods to meet the bill.   The practical effect is that B stands security to the bank for the advance made to A: and what is there in the nature of such a transaction anything worse than for one man to stand security for another in any commercial transaction ?

A great deal has been said and written about the difference between Real and Accommodation Bills : and, while no terms of admiration are too strong for the first, no terms of vituperation are too strong for the latter.   Thus, Mr. Bell says—"The difference between a genuine commercial bill and an accommodation bill is something similar to the difference between a genuine coin and a counterfeit one :" as if the fact of negotiating an Accommodation Bill were in itself one of moral turpitude

It is generally assumed that real Bills possess some sort of security because it is supposed that there is Property to represent them. We have already pointed out the error of this idea. Real and Accommodation Bills have exactly the same security—they constitute a general charge upon the whole estates of the obligants to them. The objection to Accommodation Bills, therefore, on this ground, is futile

The essential distinction between Real and Accommodation Paper is that the one represents past transactions, and the other future transactions. In a Real Bill goods have been purchased to meet the Bill : in an Accommodation Bills goods are to be purchased to meet the Bill. But this is no ground of preference for one over the other. A transaction which has been done may be just as wild, foolish, and absurd as one that has to be done. The intention of engaging in any mercantile transaction is that the result should repay the outlay with a profit. There is no other test but this of its propriety in a mercantile sense

The common objections against Accommodation Paper are, therefore, futile, and quite wide of the mark. And the proof of it is, that the largest, safest, and most profitable parts of Scotch banking are entirely of the nature of Accommodation Paper

The system of Accommodation Paper is one of immense importance in modern commerce : and its abuses have contributed to produce the greatest calamities : but, as in this part of the work, we confine ourselves to the exposition of the advantages and effects of solid Credit, we shall reserve what we have to say about the abuses of Accommodation Paper till we treat of the abuses of Credit

Exaggerated Ideas of the Security of Real Bills

5. The above are the fewest number of hands that goods in the ordinary course of business pass through, and it is clear that in their passage from the importer, or grower, to the consumer they will give two or three bills. These are all regular business bills : they originate from real transactions : and, for that reason, they are what are called **Real** or **Value** Bills. They arise out of the regular and ordinary course of business : and they are the great staple of what bankers purchase. It is a very prevalent opinion, even among men of business, that real Bills are essentially safe, because they arise out of real transactions, and always represent property. But the foregoing considerations will dispel much of the security supposed to reside in real Bills on that account : because we have seen that in the most legitimate course of business there will generally be two or three Bills afloat arising out of the transfers of any given goods : so that, in the ordinary course of business, there will be twice or thrice as many Bills afloat as there is Property to which they refer

The above operations are only what arise in the ordinary course of business : sometimes, however, goods may change hands much more frequently : and, at every transfer, a Bill may be created. In times of speculation transfers are often much more numerous : and all the Bills created on these transfers are technically real Bills : but it is evidently a delusion to suppose that there is any security in them on that account. The whole error arises from misconceiving the meaning of the word "*represent.*" A Bill of Lading does *represent* goods : because it is a title to some specific goods : and, whoever holds the Bill of Lading, has the Property in those very goods

But a Bill of Exchange does not represent any goods at all. It represents nothing but Debt : it does not even represent Money : it is nothing but a Right of action against a person to pay Money. It is created as a substitute for Money to transfer goods : but it does not represent goods any more than Money represents goods. Nor does it represent Money any more than Money represents goods : it is merely exchangeable for Money

This was long ago pointed out by Thornton[1]—" In order to justify the supposition that a real Bill, as it is called, represents actual Property, there ought to be some power in the bill holder to prevent the Property which the Bill represents from being turned to other purposes than that of paying the Bill in question.

[1] *Essay on the Paper Credit of Great Britain*

No such power exists: neither the man who holds the Bill, nor the man who discounts it, has any Property in the specific goods for which it was given "

This is perfectly manifest: the goods in which the Bill was created to transfer will probably be scattered in fifty different directions before the Bill becomes payable: and of the several Bills which are created on the repeated transfers of the goods which represents the goods? The real security of every Bill simply consists in the general ability of the parties to it to meet their engagements: and not in any specific goods or money it is supposed to represent

On the Distinction between Bills of Exchange and Bills of Lading

6. The distinction between Bills of Exchange, which are Credit, or Valuable Securities, and Bills of Lading, which are Documents of Title, is of so subtle a nature, but of such momentous consequence, that it may be well to illustrate it further

It has been shown that any amount of goods may, by repeated transfers, give rise to any number of Bills of Exchange, because a new Bill is created on each transfer, which are all *bona fide:* just for the same reason that every transfer of goods required an amount of money equal to itself to transfer it

Even supposing that the price remained the same at each transfer, it would require twenty times £20 to circulate goods to the value of £20 twenty times. But also £20 by twenty transfers will circulate goods to the value of twenty times £20. So Bills of Exchange may represent the transfers of many times the value expressed on their face. This is the case when a Bill is indorsed away for value; and the Bill represents as many additional values expressed on the face of it as there are indorsements

Thus, suppose a real transaction between A and B: A draws upon B: that represents one transaction, or transfer of goods

A then buys goods from C: C might draw upon A, in a similar way as A drew upon B. But, instead of this, A may pay for the goods he bought from C, by giving in payment for them the Bill he drew upon B. The Bill has now effected two transfers

In a similar way C may buy goods from D : and pay for then by indorsing over the Bill he has received from A. The Bill has then two indorsements and represents *three* transfers of goods

In a similar way the Bill may pass through any number of hands, and effect any number of exchanges. When C indorsed over the Bill to D, he merely sold to him the Debt which A had previously sold to him. Now that may be done either by drawing a fresh Bill on B, cancelling the first : or by simply indorsing over the Bill he received from A. Hence every indorsement is equivalent to a fresh drawing. But, if he draws a fresh Bill on B it will represent nothing but B's Debt to him : whereas, if he indorses over the Bill he received from A, it will represent B's Debt to A : A's Debt to C : and C's Debt to D : and, consequently, it will be much more desirable for D to receive a Bill which represents the sum of so many previous transactions, and for the payment of which so many parties are bound to the whole extent of their estates

This also shows that no true estimate of the effect of Bills in circulation can be formed from the returns to the Stamp Office, as has sometimes been attempted to be done : as every indorsement is in effect a new Bill. So that the useful effect of a Bill is indicated by the number of indorsements upon it

About seventy years ago the merchants of Lancashire refused to receive the notes of any private banker, and the whole Circulating Paper consisted of Bank of England Notes and Bills of Exchange, which had sometimes as many as 150 indorsements upon them before they came to maturity

But indorsements on a Bill of Lading have a totally different meaning. A Bill of Lading is bound down to the goods it represents, and always accompanies them, however many the transfers may be

Hence, ten indorsements on a Bill of Exchange denote that *eleven* times the amount of goods have been transferred *once*

Ten indorsements on a Bill of Lading denote that the *same* goods have been transferred *ten* times

On Credit Created for the purpose of forming **New Products**

7. The operations of Credit we have just considered were for the purpose of transferring commodities which had already been purchased : or which were to be purchased : but which, in either case, were already in existence. And some persons suppose that the whole purpose and limit of Credit is to transfer commodities which are already in existence

But, as Credit is an article of exchangeable property exactly like Money, it is clear that it may be applied exactly like Money to bring new products into existence. The limit of Credit in this case being exactly the same as in the former case—namely, the power of the proceeds of the work to redeem the Credit

As an example of the employment of Credit to create new products, we may quote the following instance[1]—" The States of Guernsey, having determined to build a meat market, voted £4,000 to defray the cost. Instead of borrowing this sum at 5 per cent. interest, the governor issued 4,000 cardboard tickets, on which were inscribed " Guernsey Meat Market Notes :" they represented £1 each, and were legal currency by universal consent. With these notes the States paid the contractor : and with them he paid his workmen, and all who supplied them with materials. They were freely taken by the tradesmen for goods : by landlords for rent : by the authorities for taxes. In due season the market was completed. The butcher's stalls, with some public rooms over them, were let for an annual rent of £400. At the expiration of the first year of this tenancy, the States called in the first batch of Notes, numbered 1 to 400, and, with the £400 of real money received for rent, redeemed the £400 of representative money expressed by the " Meat Market Notes." At the end of ten years all the Notes were redeemed through the application of the ten years' rental. In this way they built a very good market house without paying any interest on borrowed money, and without injuring anybody "

I am informed that one of the first docks constructed on the Banks of the Mersey, in Liverpool, was made in the same manner. Labor Notes were issued which circulated all through the town, as money does, and they were redeemed out of the dock dues of the first few years

[1] *Minton's Capital and Wages,* p. 236

Credit, being Purchasing Power, may be used to purchase Labor as well as commodities: and that Labor may be employed in forming or creating new products as well as in circulating commodities already in existence

In the next chapter we shall show that Companies have been formed on the Continent for the express purpose of promoting improvements in agriculture on this principle, and have been the main cause of the prosperity of these countries

But where institutions are very solid and enjoy high Credit, they may issue Notes, payable on demand, for the express purpose of promoting such operations. The immense improvements in agriculture, and all public works in Scotland, have been effected by the Banks issuing £1 Notes: and their £1 Notes payable in gold, on demand, are as readily received in Scotland as Money itself, and produce exactly the same effects as so much Money

Credit is, in all cases whatever, the Present Value of the future Profit: and, if it is Profitable to advance Money to effect any operation to be replaced with a profit by the result of the operation, it is, of course, equally profitable to create an equal amount of Credit, which will be redeemed with a profit by the result of the operation

CHAPTER VII

THE THEORY OF BANKING

Origin of Banking in Europe

1. The Romans invented the business which, in modern language, is termed **Banking**

At an early period Rome began to gain an ascendency over the neighbouring towns. Numerous strangers flocked to her, bringing the coins of their native towns with them. For their convenience the Government built shops round the Forum, and let them out to private persons for the purpose of exchanging the money of strangers for Roman Money. These persons were called *Argentarii:* and their shops were called *Tabernæ, Mensæ,* or *Argentariæ.* The commission they charged was called *Collybus,* from κόλλυβος, the rate of exchange for changing the money of one country for that of another. Changing money was also called *permutatio*

The business of these persons was, at first, pure money changing, but upon that they subsequently engrafted others

It became the custom of private persons to deposit their money with them for the mere purpose of security. In this case they acquired no property in the money: but they held it subject to the directions of the depositor

The money itself was termed a **Depositum**: because, in Roman Law, a *Depositum* means anything which is entrusted to the charge of another for safe custody, but in which he acquires no property. This *depositum* was in no sense a loan

The banker, not being allowed to trade with this money, paid no interest for it : and it was called *vacua pecunia.* When the depositor wished to make a payment he either gave the *argentarius* a verbal order, or gave his creditor a cheque

The *argentarii* not only received money to hold in security as a *depositum:* but they also received money as a loan which became their own Property for which they paid interest. Such money was termed a **Creditum**. The persons who placed their money with the argentarius as a **Creditum** lost all the property in it, and acquired only a Credit, Debt, or Right of action in exchange for it: which they might transfer to any one else by a Cheque

In subsequent Roman Jurisprudence, Money "lent" to a person was termed a *Mutuum*, from *mutare*, to exchange: because all "Loans" of money are exchanges

The Roman bankers also invented Bills of Exchange. Thus they invented the business which, in modern language, is termed **Banking**, *i.e.*, issuing **Credit** in exchange for specie

They, however, did not invent Bank Notes : nor is there any evidence to show that paper at any time got into general circulation as in modern times

On the Meaning of the word Bank

2. Before, however, we proceed to explain the mechanism and effects of Banking, we must ascertain the meaning of the word **Bank** : because great misconception prevails respecting it

If we take up the most common works on Banking we find it stated :—

1. That the word Bank comes from the Italian word *Banco*, which means a bench : because it is alleged that the Italian money dealers, or money changers, kept a bench on which their money was piled : whence they are said to have been called *Banchieri*

2. That the business of a banker consists in dealing in Money : or in acting as an intermediate agent between persons who want to lend money and those want to borrow money

3. That the Profits of a banker consist in the difference between the interest he pays for the money he borrows and the interest he charges for the money he lends

These statements, however, proceeding from apparently high authority, are entirely erroneous

The Italian money changers, as such, were never called*
Banchieri, in the middle ages : nor are persons whose sole
business is money changing, ever called Bankers in any language.
So long as they confined their business to money changing and
lending money they were called *Cambiatores*, *Cambitores*,
Campsores, *Speciarii*, *Argentarii*, *Nummularii*, *Trapezitæ*,
Danistæ, *Collybistæ*, and *Mutuatores* : and their places of
business were called *Casane*, and not *Banchi*

At one time there was considerable discussion in Italy as to
the origin of the word *Banco*. Many writers said that it came
from *abacus*, a calculating machine. But Muratori entirely
disapproves of such a derivation[1]—" To me, on the contrary, the
word seems to have come from the German word **Banck**, which is
a very ancient word in that language," and he says that the
word was first used for a store of goods in the town of Brescia

Ducange also says[2]—" Bank is of Franco-German or Saxon
origin : no other is to be sought for "

There is no doubt whatever that these learned authors are
right

The word Banck, in German, has two meanings—(1) a heap
or mound, like a sandbank, &c.; (2) a bench or seat. Many
writers who are not acquainted with the technicalities of
commerce suppose that the word Bank as a place of business
comes from the second of these meanings ; because they suppose
that the *banco* was the counter on which the money was placed

But the technical meaning of the word *banking :* and the
invariable use of the term by the Italian Economists, and the
universal meaning attributed to the word when it was first
introduced into English, conclusively prove that the preceding
opinion is erroneous : and that, as a technical term in commerce,
it is derived from the first of the meanings given above

The word Bank originated in this way—

The Roman State made it a cardinal maxim of their policy
not to carry on more than one war at a time. In 1171, the City
of Venice was at war both with the Empires of the East and of

[1] *Antig. Ital. Med. Æv.*, vol. ii., p. 1,148
[2] *Med. et Infin. Lat. Lex.*, Sc. 5, Bancus

the West. Its finances were in a state of great disorder, and the Great Council levied a forced loan of one per cent. on the property of all the citizens, and promised them interest at five per cent. Commissioners were appointed to manage the loan, and were called *Camera degli Imprestiti.* Such a loan has several names in Italian, such as *Compera, Mutuo, &c.:* but the most usual name is *Monte,* a joint-stock fund. This first load was called the *Monte Vecchio*—the old loan : subsequently, two other similar loans were contracted, and called the *Monte Nuovo* and *Monte Nuovissimo.* In exchange for the money the citizens received **Stock Certificates** or **Credits,** which they might transfer to any one else : and the Commissioners kept an office for the transfer of stock and the payment of the dividends

At this time the Germans were masters of a great part of Italy, and the German word **Banck,** meaning a heap, came to be used as synonymous with **Monte,** and was Italianised into **Banco:** and the public loans were called indifferently **Monti** or **Banchi**

This office was termed the Bank of Venice : and it was not, as so many writers have supposed, a Bank in the modern sense of the term : it was simply the National Debt Office : it was the origin of the Funding System

Thus, in the *Volpone* of Ben Jonson, the scene of which is laid at Venice, Volpone says—

" I turn no monies in the public Bank "

meaning " I do not dabble in the Venetian Funds "

So, an English writer, Benbrigge, in 1646, speaks of the " three **Bankes** " at Venice : meaning the three public loans or **Monti**

So, in Florio and Torriani's Italian Dictionary, published in 1659, it says—

"**Monte,** a standing *Bank* or *Mount* of money, as they have in divers cities of Italy "

That the word *Banco* in Italian means a Public Debt might be proved by numberless quotations

Thus, a recent Italian writer, Cibrario, says[1]—" Regarding the Theory of Credit, which, I have said, was invented by the Italian

[1] *Economia Politica del Medio evo.*

cities, it is known that the first **Bank** or **Public Debt** (il primo **Banco** o **Debito Pubblico**) was erected in Venice in 1171. In the thirteenth century paper money is mentioned at Milan : the Credit was paid off. A Monte or Public Debt (un **Monte** o **Debito Pubblico**) was founded at Florence in 1336 . . . .

At Genoa, during the wars of the fourteenth century, the **Bank** of St. George, was founded formed of the Creditors of the State "

Every Economist in the south of Europe knows that the word **Banco** means a **Public Debt**

Thus the distinguished Spanish Economist Olozaga, speaking of the Venetian loans, says[1]—" el Monte Vecchio (banco viejo) . . . . . el Monte Nuevo (banco nuevo) "

So in Barretti's Italian Dictionary, 1839, it says—" **Monte**, a bank where they lend or take money at interest "

So Evelyn speaks[2] of the " *Monte di Pietà*," at Padua, where there is a continual Bank of Money to assist the poor "

So Blackstone says[3]—" At Florence in 1344 Government owed £60,000, and being unable to pay it, formed the principal into an aggregate sum called metaphorically a **Mount** or **Bank** "

Every one who is acquainted with the writings of the Italian Economists knows perfectly well that they invariably use the words *Monti* and *Banchi* as absolutely synonymous : and in the Reports published by the Statistical Office of Italy, the words are also used as synonymous

This was also the meaning of the word **Bank** when it was first introduced into English

Thus Bacon says[4]—" Let it be no **Bank** or common stock "

So Gerard Malynes says[5]—" *Mons Pietatis* or Bank of Charity." " In Italy there are *Montes Pietatis* ; that is to say, Mounts or Banks of Charity "

Benbrigge, in his Usura Accommodata, in 1646, says—" For their rescue may be collected *Mons Pietatis sive Charitatis*, or Banke of Piety or Charity, as they of Trent fitly call it "

[1] *Tratado de Economía Política*, vol. i., p. 101
[2] *Diary*, vol. i., p. 101
[3] Vol. i., p. 322, Kerr's Edit.
[4] *Essay on Usury*   [5] *Lex Mercatoria*, Part ii., ch. 13

Again—"For borrowers in trade for their supply as their occasion shall require may be erected *Mons Negotiationis* or Banke of Trade"

Tolet says—"*Mons fidei*, a Banke of Trust which Clement XII. instituted at Rome—he that put his money into this Banke was never to take it out again," for which the lender received 7 per cent. interest, like the subscribers to the original Bank of England stock. He also speaks of *Mons Recuperationis*, or Banke of Recovery, in which the interest was 12 per cent.

The difference between these two, which were Public Debts, was, the first was a perpetual annuity, and the second a terminable annuity

In the time of Cromwell several proposals were made for erecting public Banks. Samuel Lambe, a London merchant, in 1658, recommending them, says—"A Bank is a certain number of sufficient men of estates and credit joined together in Joint Stock : being as it were the general cash keepers, or treasurers of that place where they are settled, letting out imaginary money, (*i.e.*, Credit) at interest at £2½ or £3 per cent. to tradesmen, or others that agree with them for the same, and making payment thereof by assignation, and passing each man's account from one to another with much facility and ease"

So Francis Cradocke, a London merchant, who was appointed a member of the Board of Trade by Charles II. strongly advocated the introduction of Banks into England, says—"A Banke is a certain number of sufficient men of Credit joyned together in a stock, as it were, for keeping several men's cash in one Treasury, and letting out imaginary money, (*i.e.*, Credit) at interest for three or more in the hundred per annum, to tradesmen or others that agree with them for the same : and making payment thereof by assignation, passing each man's account from one to another, yet paying little money." And he says that "the aforesaid bankers may furnish another petty Bank (or Mount) of Charity"

Thus these writers perfectly understood the nature and constitution of a Bank

In a little tract, entitled "*A Discourse concerning Banks*," published in 1697, and supposed to be by a director of the Bank of England, it says, "that there are three kinds of Banks: the first for the mere Deposit of money, the second for profit." "The Banks of the second kind, called in Italy **Monti**, which are for the benefit of the income only, are the Banks of Rome, Bolonia, and Milan. These Banks are made up of a number of persons who in time of war, or other exigencies of state, advanced sums of money upon funds granted *in perpetuum*, but redeemable. . . The third kind of Banks, which are both for the convenience of the public, and the advantage of the undertakers, are the several Banks of Naples, the Bank of St. George at Genoa, and one of the Banks of Bolonia. These Banks having advanced sums of money at their establishment, did not only agree for a fund of perpetual interest, but were allowed the privilege of keeping cash "

The Bank of England was of this last kind. It was a company of persons who advanced a sum of money to Government, and received in exchange for it a perpetual annuity: or a Right to a series of payments for ever from the State. This annuity in popular language is termed the Funds: but its legal name is " **Bank Annuities** "

There has only been one instance in this country of a Bank which did not receive cash from the public. Some time after the foundation of the Bank of England a company of persons united to advance a million to the Government. They were incorporated as the " Million Bank." This company existed till nearly the end of the last century: and thus it resembled the original Bank of Venice

Thus from these passages, and an infinitely larger number might be given if necessary, it is perfectly clear that the word Bank, as a term in commerce, is the equivalent of **Monte**: and means a joint stock fund contributed by a number of persons

The essential feature of all these Banks was this: the subscribers advanced the Money as a Loan or *Mutuum:* it thus becomes the actual property of the borrowers: and in exchange for their money the lenders received a Credit, *i.e.*, a certificate or promise to pay interest, which they might transfer to any one else

And those persons whose business it was to trade like these Banks, *i.e.*, to buy money, and in exchange for it to issue Credit of various sorts, were termed **Bankers**, and only those

Thus as a technical term in business, to "**Bank**" means to issue **Credit**

On the Meaning *of the word* Banker

3. Equally great misconception prevails as to the meaning of the word Banker and the nature of the business of Banking

Gilbart says[1]—" A banker is a dealer in Capital : or, more properly, a dealer in **Money**. He is an intermediate party between the borrower and the lender. He borrows of one party and lends to another : and the difference between the terms at which he borrows, and those at which he lends, forms the source of his profit"

So a report of the House of Commons says[2]—" The use of Money and that only they regard as the province of a bank, whether of a private person, or Incorporation, or the banking department of the Bank of England "

Notwithstanding the apparent authority of these passages which have misled so many unwary persons ; these descriptions of banking are utterly erroneous

In former times there were many persons who acted as intermediaries between persons who wanted to lend and those who wanted to borrow. They were called Money Scriveners. The father of John Milton was a Money Scrivener. But no one ever called a Money Scrivener a Banker

At the present day many firms of solicitors act as intermediaries between persons who wish to lend and others who wish to borrow. They may have some clients who wish to borrow, and other clients who wish to lend : and they act as agents between them. The second set may entrust their money to the firm to lend to the first set : and the solicitors receive a commission on the sums which pass through their hands

But no one ever called a firm of solicitors who transact such agency business **Bankers** : which shows that there is an essential distinction between the business of such solicitors and the business of Banking

[1] *Principles of Banking*, p. 1   [2] *Report on Commercial Distress*, 1858

Solicitors who transact such agency business do not acquire any Property in the money which passes through their hands. They receive it merely as a **Depositum** or **Bailment** : they are only the Custodians or Trustees of the money: and it is only entrusted to their custody for the express purpose of being applied in a certain way. The actual property in the money passes directly from the lender to the borrower through the medium of the Trustees or Bailees : and if the latter appropriated it in any way to their own purposes, they would be liable to be punished for embezzlement

But the case of a **Banker** is wholly different. When his customers pay in money to their account, they cede the Property in the money to the Banker. The money placed with him is not a **Depositum** or **Bailment**: but it is a **Mutuum**: it is a loan or sale of the money directly to himself. The banker is not the Trustee or Bailee of the money but its actual **Proprietor.** The banker buys the money from his customer : and in exchange for it, he gives his customer a Credit in his books, which is a Right of action to demand back an equivalent amount of money at any time he pleases : and the customer may also transfer this Right of action to any one else he pleases

When, therefore, the client of a solicitor entrusts money to him to lend to some one else, he retains the Property in it until the arrangement with the borrower is completed : and then the Property in the money is transferred direct from the lender to the borrower ; without even vesting in the solicitor. But when a customer pays in money to his account at his banker's the Property in the money instantly and *ipso facto* vests in the banker : and the customer has nothing but a Right of action against the person of the banker to demand back an equivalent sum

Galiani says[1]—" Banks began when men saw, from experience that there was not sufficient money in specie for great commerce and great enterprises "

" The first banks were in the hands of private persons with whom persons deposited money : and from whom they received

[1] *Della Moneta*, p. 323

Bills of Credit (*fedi di credito*) : and who were governed by the same rules as the public banks now are.   And thus the Italians have been not only the fathers and the masters, and the arbiters of commerce, so that in all Europe they have been the depositories of money, and are called Bankers"

So Genovesi says[1]—"These Monti were at first administered with scrupulous fidelity, as were all human institutions made in the heat of virtue.   From which it came to pass that many placed their money on deposit : and, as a security, received Paper which was called, and is still called, Bills of Credit"

"Thus private banks were established among us, whose Bills of Credit acquired a great circulation, and increased the quantity of signs and the velocity of commerce"

And this was always recognised as the essential feature of "Banking"

Thus Marquardus says[2]—"And by "Banking" is meant a certain species of trading in money, under the sanction of public authority, in which money is placed with bankers (who are also cashiers and depositories of money) for the security of Creditors and the convenience of Debtors in such a way that *the Property in the money passes to them:* but always with the condition understood that any one who places his money with them may have it back whenever he pleases"

A "Banker" is therefore a person who trades in the way that the Public Banks did : they acquired the Property in the money paid in : and in exchange for it they gave **Bills of Credit**, which circulated in commerce exactly like money, and produced all the effects of money.   And moreover when they bought or discounted Bills of Exchange, they did it exactly in the same way : they bought them with their own **Credit:** and *not* with Money.   And experience showed that they might multiply their Bills of Credit several times exceeding the quantity of money they held : and thus for all practical purposes multiply the quantity of money in circulation

Thus the essential business of a " Banker " is to create **Credit**

The following is the true definition of a " Banker "

[1] *Delle Lezioni di Economica Civile*, Part ii., ch. 5, § 5
[2] *De Jure Mercatorum*, Lib. ii., ch. 12, § 13

A **Banker** *is a Trader whose business is to* buy **Money** *and* **Debts** *by creating other* **Debts**

As will be more fully exemplified in subsequent sections

On the Currency Principle

4. We must now explain the meaning of an expression which has acquired much importance, and which must be clearly understood before we come to the exposition of the system which the Bank Charter Act of 1844 was designed to carry out

The express function and purpose of a Bank being to create Credit, it has sometimes been maintained that a Bank should only be allowed to create exactly as much credit as the specie paid in and no more. And that its sole function should be to exchange Credit for Money and Money for Credit : and thus the quantity of Credit in circulation would always be exactly equal to the Money it displaced

This doctrine is that which is distinctively known by the name of the "**Currency Principle**:" it is the doctrine which the supporters of the Bank Act of 1844 asserted to be the only true one : and which that Act was specially designed to carry out

This doctrine is supposed to be of modern origin, and the latest refinement in the Theory of Banking. But this is far from being the case : it was first formulated in China in 1309

That country had been plagued for 500 years with the excessive issues of inconvertible paper by the banks. The author of a work *Tsoa-min* exhibiting the evil consequences of excessive issues of Paper Money, and speaking of the times before such mischief arose, said—"Then it was ordered that at the offices of the rich merchants who managed the enterprise, when the Notes were paid in the Money came out : when the Bills came out the Money went in : the Money was the mother, the Note was the son. The son and the mother were reciprocally exchanged for the other"

Several Banks have been constructed on this principle : such as those of Venice, Amsterdam, Hamburg, Nuremberg, and others

These places, small in themselves, were the centres of a great foreign commerce : and as a necessary consequence large quantities of foreign coin of all sorts, of different countries and denominations were brought by the foreigners who resorted to them. These coins were, moreover, greatly clipped, worn, and diminished. The degraded state of the current coin produced intolerable inconvenience, disorder, and confusion among merchants, who, when they paid or received payment of their bills had to offer or receive a bagful of all sorts of different coins. The settlement of these bills, therefore, involved perpetual disputes—which coins were to be received and which were not, and how much each was to count for

In order to remedy this intolerable inconvenience, it became necessary to institute some fixed and uniform standard of payment, so as to insure regularity of payments, and a just discharge of debts

To effect this purpose the magistrates of these cities instituted a Bank of Deposit, into which every merchant paid his coin of all sorts and countries. These were weighed, and the Bank gave him credit in its books for the exact bullion value of the coins paid in. The owner of the credit was entitled to have it paid in full weighted coin on demand

These Credits, therefore, insured a uniform standard of payment and were called Bank Money—*Moneta di Banco*: and it was enacted that all bills upon these cities above a certain small amount should be paid in Bank Money only

As this Bank Money was always exchangeable for coin at full weight on demand, it was always at a premium, or *agio*, as compared with the worn, clipped, and degraded coin in circulation. The difference was usually from 5 to 9 per cent., in the different cities. The term *agio* is misleading ; because it is clear that it was the *Moneta di Banco* that was the full legal standard : and the current coin was at a discount

These Banks professed to keep all the coin and bullion deposited with them in their vaults. They made no use of it in the way of business, as by discounting bills. Thus the Credit created was exactly equal to the specie deposited : and their sole function was to exchange Credit for specie and specie for Credit

These Banks were examples of the **Currency Principle.** They were of no use to commerce further than to serve as a safe place to keep the money of the merchants, and to insure a uniform standard for the payment of Debts. They made no profits by their business : and no Bank constructed on the Currency Principle can by any possibility make profits. The merchants who kept their accounts with the Bank paid certain fees to defray the expenses of the establishment

These Banks were called Banks of Deposit : but they were not Banks in the true sense of the word, because the money deposited with them did not become their absolute property to deal with as they pleased. They were simply Trustees of the money. They were not the Bankers, but the Treasurers of the merchants, and were obliged to take a solemn oath they would keep in their vaults all the money placed with them. Nevertheless, both at Venice and Amsterdam they violated their solemn oaths, and advanced large sums to the Government, which ultimately led to their ruin

On the Mechanism of Banking

5. Banks of the nature of those of Venice, Amsterdam, Hamburg, Nuremberg, and others, founded on the Currency Principle never existed in this country : and we must now explain the mechanism of the great system of Banking, or the great system of the commerce in Debts, Credits, or Rights of action, as it has been carried on in this country

It was during the great civil war, as we have explained elsewhere, that the goldsmiths of London first began to receive the cash of the merchants and country gentlemen for safe custody, on condition of repaying an equal sum on demand : and to discount Bills of Exchange : that is, commenced the Business of Banking

Now this money was not placed in their hands to be locked away idle in their cellars, as plate and jewelry are often given into the custody of a banker for mere safe custody as a *Depositum*, and to be restored *in specie*. The money was sold to the banker to become his actual property according to the well understood custom of bankers : that is, it was a **Mutuum** : and to be restored only *in genere*. The goldsmith bankers agreed not only to repay the money on demand : but also to pay six per cent. interest for it. Consequently, in order to make a profit, they were obliged to trade with it

We must now explain how a banker makes a profit by the money his customers sell to him

Suppose that customers pay in £10,000 to their accounts : they cede the absolute property in the money to the banker : it is a **Mutuum**. The banker buys the money from his customers : and, in exchange for it, he gives them an equal amount of Credit in his books : that is, he creates Rights of action against himself to an equal amount : giving his customers the right to demand back an equivalent sum of money at any time they please : and also the right of transferring their Rights of action to any one else they please : exactly as if they were money : and the banker engages to pay the Transferee the same as his own customer

This Right of action, Credit, or Debt, entered in the banker's books is, in banking language, technically termed a **Deposit**

After such an operation his accounts would stand thus—

LIABILITIES.		ASSETS.	
Deposits	£10,000	Cash	£10,000

Now though his customers have Rights of action against the banker to demand back exactly an equal sum of money to what they have paid in : yet persons would not pay money to their banker if they meant to draw it out again immediately ; just as no one would spend all the money he has at once

Nevertheless, some will want to draw out part of their funds : but, if some customers want to draw out money, others will probably pay in about an equal sum. Observation shows that in ordinary and quiet times a banker's balance in cash will seldom differ by more than one thirty-sixth part from day to day

The banker's cash is therefore like a column of gold with a slight ripple on the surface : and if he retains one-tenth in cash to meet any demands which may be made upon him, that is ample and abundant in all ordinary times

If, then, in the above example the banker retains £1,000 in cash to meet any demands upon him, he has £9,000 to trade with and make a profit by : and it is just in the method in which bankers trade that so much misconception exists

It is commonly supposed that when a banker has the £9,000 to trade with he employs it in purchasing Bills of Exchange to that amount : and that he receives a profit only on the £9,000 : but that is a complete misconception of the nature of **Banking**

A " Banker " never buys Bills of Exchange with Money : that is the business of a bill discounter : or a bill broker

The way in which a "Banker" trades is this : he sees that £1,000 in cash is sufficient to support £10,000 of Liabilities in Credit : consequently he argues that £10,000 in cash will bear Liabilities to several times that amount in Credit

One of the most eligible methods of trading for a Banker is to buy, or discount, good Commercial Bills. And he buys these Bills exactly in the same way as he bought the Cash : that is, by creating Credits in his books : or Debts : or Rights of action against himself to the amount of the Bills—deducting at the same time the Interest, or Profit, agreed upon : which is called the Discount

A "Banker" therefore invariably buys a Bill with his own **Credit**: and never with Cash—exactly in the same way as he bought the Cash. That is, he buys a Right of action payable at a future time by issuing a Right of action, payable on demand, and this Right of action, or Credit is equally in banking language termed a **Deposit** : as the Right of action created and issued to buy the cash

Suppose that the Banker buys £40,000 of Commercial Bills at three months, and that the agreed upon Profit is four per cent. then the sum to be retained on these Bills is £400. Consequently in exchange for Bills to the amount of £40,000 he would create Credits, Debts, Rights of action—technically termed **Deposits**—to the amount of £39,600

Hence just after discounting these Bills and before his customers begin to operate on their accounts, his accounts would stand thus—

LIABILITIES.			ASSETS.		
Deposits ..	..	.. £49,600	Cash ..	..	.. £10,000
			Bills of Exchange	..	40,000
		£49,600			£50,000

The balance of £400 being his own Property, or Profit

By this process the "Banker" has added £39,600 in Credit to the previously existing cash : and his Profit is clear : he has not gained four per cent. on the £9,000 in cash : but four per cent. on the £40,000 of Bills he has bought

This is what the business of Banking essentially consists in : and thus the correctness of the definition of a "Banker" given above is manifest

Thus we see that the very essence and nature of a **Bank** and a **Banker** : is to create and issue Credit payable on demand : and this Credit is intended to Circulate and perform all the purposes of money

A Bank is, therefore, not an office for "borrowing" and "lending" money : but it is a **Manufactory of Credit**: as Bishop Berkeley said, "a **Bank is a Gold Mine**"

On the Legal Relation *between* Banker *and* Customer

6. It must be carefully observed that the **Legal Relation** between Banker and Customer is simply that of Debtor and Creditor

When a customer pays in money to his account he cedes the absolute property in the money to the banker, and receives in exchange an abstract Right of action to demand an equivalent sum of money, but not the identical money

In speaking of banking, it is too often implied that the money placed with the banker still belongs to the customer. But this was decisively refuted by Lord Chancellor Cottenham[1]

It must, therefore, be carefully observed that a Banker in no way resembles the Treasurer of a public fund, or a solicitor, or a money scrivener, who are only Trustees of the money in their custody. If a banker were the mere Trustee of the money placed with him he would have no right to use it for his own purposes

It is often the custom of persons to say that they have so much "Money" at their banker's : but such an expression is

[1] *Foley* v. *Hill* (2 H. L. cases, 28)

wholly erroneous and misleading: they have no "Money" at their banker's: they have nothing but an abstract **Right of action** to demand so much money from their banker

As a consequence of this relation between banker and customer, if a customer were to leave a balance at his banker's for six years without operating on it, the banker might, if he chose to be so dishonest, refuse to pay it under the Statute of Limitations: just like any other ordinary debt. But if it were a mere Trust he could not refuse to pay it: because the Statute of Limitations does not apply to Trusts

Another consequence of this relation is that a Cheque is a Bill of Exchange and not a Draft: it is an order addressed by a Creditor to his Debtor: and not one addressed by a person to his Trustee or Bailee. To call a Cheque a Draft is to mistake the relation between Banker and Customer

On the Legal Contract between Banker and Customer

7. It has been shown that the Legal Relation between Banker and Customer is simply that of Debtor and Creditor

Nevertheless, there is an important distinction between an ordinary Debtor and a Banker Debtor

At Common Law an ordinary Debtor is not bound to accept a bill drawn upon him by his Creditor without his own consent: even though he admits the Debt: nor if his Creditor assigns the Debt is he bound to pay the Transferee: nor has the Transferee an action against him in his own name: because there is no privity of contract between the Debtor and the Transferee: and the Creditor has no power to stipulate that his Debtor shall pay the Transferee: unless he expressly consents to do so

The Transferee can only sue the Debtor under the name of the Transferor: or the Transferor can sue the Debtor as the Trustee of the Transferee

If, however, the Debtor had entered into an Obligation under seal promising to pay the assignee or bearer: or if he had accepted a Bill payable to order, or to bearer: then the Transferee might sue him in his own name: because the consent of the Debtor had created a privity of contract between himself and the Transferee

But the case of a Banker Debtor has always been different. In order to encourage persons to place their money with them, the Goldsmith Bankers agreed that their customers should have exactly the same facilities for transferring their Rights of action, as if they had the Money itself in their hands

Consequently, from the very first institution of Banking, it was always the custom of bankers that the customers might either demand payment themselves : or they might transfer their Rights of action to any one they pleased, or to order, or to bearer

By the very nature, therefore, of the Consensual Contract, called the Custom of Bankers, a banker having funds of his customer is in the position of an ordinary Debtor who has accepted a bill payable to order, or to bearer

Hence, while the simple admission of the possession of funds by an ordinary Debtor in no way compels him to accept or pay a bill drawn on him, without his own consent : the simple admission of the possession of funds by a banker operates, *ipso facto*, as a legal acceptance of any Bills or Cheques drawn upon him by his customer : and gives the holders of them a Right of action against him

It had long been held at the Bar that the holder of a Cheque has no action against a banker, even though he possesses funds of his customer, because he has not accepted the Cheque

But in the work I did for the Law Digest Commission I established that the true doctrine of the Common Law is that when a person, either orally or in writing, creates an Obligation transferable to order or to bearer he is liable to an action by the Transferee.   And this doctrine received the unanimous assent of the Commissioners; and was afterwards unanimously affirmed by the Court of Exchequer Chamber in the great case of *Goodwin* v. *Robarts*

When therefore it was held at the bar and in the text books of Mercantile Law that the holder of a Cheque has no action against a banker, the radical difference between an ordinary Debtor and a Banker Debtor was overlooked. By the fundamental contract between banker and customer the banker has given his consent that his customer may transfer his Right of action to any one else he pleases : and this is further evidenced by the very form of the Cheques delivered to him, which are expressly made payable to order or to bearer. Consequently, if the holder can prove that the banker has funds of his customer, he has an action against him

Martin, B., said[1]—"A banker is in the position of a person having in his hands the money of another, which he is at any moment liable to pay : and the Courts have grasped at that to make a contract between the banker, his customer, and a third party, for the payment of the money to the latter operates as a transfer of the money, so that an action for money had and received can be maintained for it"

The fact is that it is not the Courts which have made the contract, but they only enforce the fundamental contract between banker and customer which the decision in *Goodwin* v. *Robarts* has declared to be a perfectly legal one

This point, however, has less importance now, because by the Supreme Court of Judicature the rules of Equity are now established as Law, and the holder of a Cheque could always sue a banker in equity if he could prove that the banker held sufficient funds of his customer to meet the Cheque ; which completely settles and determines any doubt that there might previously have been on the subject

On the Meaning of Deposit *in the technical language of modern Banking*

8. The word **Depositum** is one of that class of Latin words, of which we have seen several instances already, which in classical and even in juridical Latin meant a material thing, but which in modern times has come to mean an abstract Right

A *Depositum* in Roman Law means anything which is placed in the gratuitous charge or custody of some person for the sole purpose of safe keeping : without the property in it passing to him ; or his being allowed to use it in any way for his own advantage : he was not even allowed to retain it as a security for a debt due to him

It is a part of the duty of a London banker to take charge of his customers' plate, jewelry and securities if required to do so. This plate, jewelry, and securities so committed to their charge is what is called in Roman Law a *Depositum*

[1] *Liversidge* v. *Broadbent* (4 H. & N., 612)

The banker acquires no property in such a *Depositum :* he can make no use of it for his advantage : he receives no remuneration for keeping it : and he has even no lien upon it if his customer should become indebted to him

So if a customer tied up a sum of money in a bag and placed it in the custody of his banker it would be a *Depositum :* and the banker would be bound to re-deliver the specific bag of money to him on demand, untouched

It is almost universally supposed by lay writers, that when a customer pays in money to his account with his banker's that it is a **Deposit ;** and it is supposed that the Deposits in a bank are the cash held in reserve. This, however, is a pure delusion. The money paid in by a customer to a bank is not a *Depositum :* it is a *Mutuum*

If the money so paid in were a *Depositum* it would mean that the banker acquired no property in it : that the property in it remained in the customer who placed it in his banker's hands for pure safe keeping : and that the customer could demand back the specific sum of money at any time he pleased

But when a customer pays in money to his account in the usual way of business he sells it to the banker. It becomes the banker's own property to deal with in any way he pleases. The customer loses all property in it, and what he acquires in exchange for the money is a Right of action to demand back an equivalent sum of money, but not the identical money. The money, therefore, so paid in is therefore a *Mutuum :* and not a *Depositum*

In exchange for the money the banker makes an entry of an equal sum in Credit in favor of his customer. And it is the entry to the Credit of the customer which, in the technical language of modern banking is termed a **Deposit**

A **Deposit,** therefore, in banking language, is not the cash in reserve : but the **Liability** of the banker to pay a sum of money on demand

So when a banker discounts a bill for a customer he buys it exactly in the same way as he bought money from his customer. He creates a credit in his books in favour of his customer. And this Credit created to purchase the bill is termed a **Deposit** equally as the Credit created to purchase the money. The money and the bills are the banker's Assets.   The Deposits are the Rights of action he has created to purchase his Assets.   Every advance a banker makes is done by creating a Deposit.   His Depositors are those persons who have Rights of action against him to pay money, or his Creditors.   A **Deposit** is simply a **Banking Credit**

In Banking Language a **Deposit** *and an* **Issue** *are the same*

9. It must therefore be carefully observed that in the technical language of modern banking a **Deposit** and an **Issue** are the same thing.   A Deposit is simply a Credit in the banker's books. It is the evidence of the Right of action which a customer has to demand a sum of money from the banker.   As soon as the banker has created a Credit, or Deposit, in his books in favor of a customer he has **Issued** to him a Right of action against himself

The word **Issue** comes from *Exitus*, a going forth : and, in Mercantile Law, to issue an Instrument is to deliver it to any one so as to give him a Right of action against the deliverer

It in no way increases the banker's liability to write down this Credit or Deposit in the form of a Bank Note or Cheque.   Such is only done for the convenience of transferring the Credit to some one else

Bank Notes and Cheques, then, do not increase a banker's liability.   The liability is created as soon as the banker has entered the amount to his customer's credit in his books.   The Note or Cheque is merely a convenient method of transferring the pre-created liability which has already been issued

Deposits, then, instead of being so much cash, as is so commonly supposed, are nothing but the Credits or Rights of action the banker has created as the price to purchase the Cash and Bills which figure on the other side of the account as his assets.   A sudden increase of Deposits is, therefore, nothing more than an inflation of Credit, exactly similar to a sudden increase of Bank notes.   Deposits are nothing but Bank Notes in disguise

A very sudden increase of Deposits is as sure a symptom of danger as a very sudden increase of Bank Notes. It has been invariably observed that all the great Commercial Crises in modern times have been preceded by very sudden increases of Deposits. And after these Monetary panics had passed away it has been invariably observed that banking Deposits greatly diminished

This has often been attributed to persons withdrawing their balances at such periods. But such assertions are erroneous. The banks have then just as much cash as at other times : probably more. But the decrease of Deposits arises from the fact that after commercial catastrophes many of the customers who discounted bills were ruined. Consequently in the depression of commerce fewer bills are created. There are, therefore, fewer bills offered for sale to the banks : and if they have fewer bills to discount, they, of course, cannot create Deposits. Hence a diminution of Deposits is not necessarily a diminution of cash, but it is a **Contraction of Credit**

On the Method of Utilising Banking Credits

10. The banker, then, having issued these Credits, Deposits, or Rights of action against himself to his customers, they cannot, of course, transfer them by manual delivery in that form to any one else. In order to be capable of manual delivery they must be recorded on paper or any other material

And this might be done in two forms—

1. The banker might give his customer his own Promissory Notes promising to pay a certain sum to his customer or to his order, or to bearer on demand

2. The customer might write a note to his banker directing him to pay a certain sum to a certain person, or to his order, or to bearer on demand. These orders were formerly called Cash Notes : but they are now termed Cheques

These paper documents do not create new liabilities : they merely record on paper the Debts, Credits, or Deposits which have already been created in the banker's books : and their sole use is to facilitate the transfer of these Rights of action to other persons

Now there are certain juridical distinctions between Bank Notes and Cheques: as, for instance, a Note is the absolute obligation to pay it: whereas a Cheque is only the contingent obligation to pay in the event of the customer having sufficient credit on his account to meet it, which leads to certain practical distinctions between Notes and Cheques: but, so far as regards Economics, Notes and Cheques are absolutely identical; and they are equally **Circulating Medium, or Currency**

Bankers' Notes were at first merely written on paper like any other promissory notes, and they were for any sums the customer might require. In 1729, Child & Co. introduced the practice of having their Notes partly printed and partly written like a modern Cheque. They were not like modern notes for fixed definite sums: but like modern cheques for any sum that might be required

London bankers appear to have issued their own notes till about 1793: when perhaps the panic of that year may have shown them the danger of having large amounts of their notes in the hands of the public. Of their own accord they discontinued issuing notes: but they were never forbidden to do so until the Bank Act of 1844

Most erroneous conclusions have been drawn from the fact of the London bankers having voluntarily discontinued issuing their own notes. Lay writers, who know nothing of the mechanism of banking, have asserted that the London banks are like the Banks of Venice, Amsterdam, &c., pure banks of deposit: that they do not create Credit: and that their whole business is to "lend" out the money they "borrow" from their customers. Such ideas, however, are pure delusions. Bankers now make all their advances by creating Credits or Deposits in their books. But instead of giving their customers two methods of circulating these Credits by means either of Notes or Cheques, they are now exclusively circulated by Cheques. But whether a Credit is circulated by means of a Note or Cheque can make no possible difference in Economics

Nevertheless, the discontinuance of issuing notes by the London bankers has had one immensely important practical consequence which they never foresaw. After it was shown by an experience of thirty years that banking could be carried on without issuing notes : some lynx-eyed Economists began to scrutinize the privileges of the Bank of England : and they maintained that its monopoly was restricted to the power of issuing notes : and that Joint-Stock Banks might be founded, which, like the private bankers, did not issue notes. This view was found to be correct : and the result was the formation of the London Joint-Stock Banks, as will be more fully described hereafter

The Bank Charter Act of 1844 allowed the Banks which were then issuing notes to continue to do so to a certain limited amount : but forbade any new bank to commence doing so. A considerable number of the banks which issued notes in 1844 having disappeared, the notes of private bankers in England have diminished by some millions. Many ill-informed writers have drawn the conclusion from this circumstance that the currency of the country has been so much diminished. This, however, is a pure delusion. The system of banking has enormously increased since then, and the amount of Banking Credits has increased by scores of millions : and these increased Banking Credits being circulated by Cheques are **Currency** in exactly the same way as **Notes**

Operations by means of Notes and Cheques

When, therefore, a banker has created a Credit or Deposit in favour of his customer, he can put this Credit into circulation either by means of the banker's own Note or by means of a Cheque : and when he does so the following different results may take place :—

1. The customer himself, or the holder of the Note or Cheque, may demand payment of it : if they do so the banker's liability is extinguished. It is a re-sale of money to the holder of the Note or Cheque : and the banker buys up the Right of action against himself

2. The Note or Cheque may circulate in commerce, and effect any number of transfers of commodities or payments exactly like an equal sum of money : and it may ultimately fall into the hands of a customer of the same bank, who pays it into his own account, and the whole series of transactions is finally closed by the mere transfer of Credit from the account of the drawer to that of the holder, without the necessity of any coin

3. The Note or Cheque may, after performing a similar series of operations, fall into the hands of a customer of another bank. So the banker becomes debtor to the customer of another bank

But if the bank A becomes debtor to the customers of bank B, the chances are that about an equal number of the customers of bank A will have about equal claims against bank B. If the mutual claims of the customers of each bank are exactly equal the respective documents are interchanged, and the Credits are re-adjusted among the accounts of the different customers without any payment in money. Thus if the mutual claims among any number of bankers exactly balanced, any amount of Credits, however large, might be settled without the use of a single coin

Formerly, if the mutual claims did not balance, the differences only used to be paid in Money or Bank Notes. But now, by an ingenious arrangement of the Clearing House, which will be described shortly, the use of coin and bank notes is entirely dispensed with : and all the banks which join in the clearing are really and practically formed into one huge banking institution for the purpose of transferring Credits among each other : just as Credits are usually transferred from one account to another in the same bank : without a single coin being required

Error of the Common Description of Banking

11. From the preceding account of the actual mechanism of Banking, it will be seen what a complete misconception of its nature it is to say that bankers are merely agents or intermediaries between persons who wish to lend and those who wish to borrow

This is entirely untrue in the ordinary sense of "lending" and "borrowing": because in the ordinary case of lending the "lender" deprives himself of the use of the thing "lent"

But when a person pays in money to his banker, he has no intention of depriving himself of the use of it. On the contrary, he means to have the same free command of it as if he had it in his own house. The customer, therefore, "lends" his money to his banker, but at the same time has the free use of it. The banker employs that money in promoting trade. Upon the strength of having acquired it he buys Debts with his promises to pay, several times exceeding the amount of money he possesses: and the persons who sell him their debts, have the free use of the very same coin which the lenders have the same right to demand. Thus the "lenders" and the "borrowers" have the same rights to demand the same coin at the same time. And all banking depends on the calculation that only a certain portion of each set of customers will demand the actual cash: but that the majority will be satisfied with the mere promise to pay, or the Credit

The whole of this mystery and confusion is cleared away by simply observing that a Bank is merely a shop for the sale of Credit, and the quantity of Credit which a Bank can create, is determined by the ratio of the Demand for payment in money compared to the total quantity of Credit created

Banking is a species of insurance: it entirely depends on the doctrine of chances: it is practically possible that a banker may be called upon to pay all his liabilities on demand at once: just as it is theoretically possible that all the lives insured in an office may drop at the same instant: and it is theoretically possible that all the houses in an office may be burned down at the same instant

A large and sudden demand for money on a Bank is termed a Run: and a Run upon a Bank is analogous to a pestilence or a conflagration to an Insurance Office. But all Insurance and Banking is based upon the expectation that these contingencies will not happen. A banker *multiplies* his liabilities to pay on demand, and keeps by him a sufficient amount of cash to insure the immediate payment of all claims which are likely to be

demanded at one time.   If a pressure comes upon him he must
sell some of the securities he has bought, or borrow money upon
them

Contrast *between the* Common Notions *about Banking and the* Reality

12.   Having now given an exposition of the actual facts and
mechanism of Banking, it will be as well to contrast the Common
Notions respecting it with the Reality

I.   It is commonly supposed that Bankers are dealers in
Money only: that they borrow Money from one set of persons
and lend it to another set

The fact is that Bankers are **not** dealers in Money: they
never lend Money.   The sole function of a Bank is to create and
Issue Credit: and to buy Money and Debts by creating and
Issuing other Debts

II.   It is commonly supposed that Bankers act only as
agents or intermediaries between persons who want to lend and
those who want to borrow

Bankers never act as agents between those who want to lend
and those who want to borrow.   Bankers buy money from some
persons: and Rights of action from others: exclusively with
their own Credit

III.   It is commonly supposed that a Banker's profit consists
in the Difference between the interest he pays for the Money he
borrows, and the Interest he charges for the Money he lends

The fact is, that a Banker's profits consist exclusively in the
profits he can make, by creating and issuing Credit in excess of
the specie he holds in reserve

No Bank which issues Credit only in exchange for Money
ever did, or by any possibility could make profits.   It only
begins to make profits when it creates and issues Credit in excess
of the Credit it issues in exchange for Money: in buying Debts
payable at a future time: which, according to Mill, as we shall
see hereafter, is robbery !

How Credit *is* Capital *to a* Banker

13.   It is now seen how Credit is Capital to a Banker

For what is the commodity a banker deals in ? He opens his place of business and has an array of clerks, with their desks, ledgers, &c. He then gives notice that he is ready to buy gold from any one who has it to sell. And what does he buy the gold with ? His own **Credit**. His own Credit is the Commodity which he gives in exchange for the Gold

He then gives notice that he is ready to buy good Commercial Debts—which are Credit—which any one has got to sell. And what does he buy these Credits with ? Again, nothing but his own Credit. His own Credit is the Commodity with which he buys these other Credits

The banker charges exactly the same price for his Credit as if it were Money. The only Commodity then the banker has to sell is his own Credit. He charges exactly the same price for his Credit as if it were Money. Hence, he makes exactly the same Profit by selling his Credit as if he were selling Money

Now, as we have seen that Anything which gives a Profit is Capital. Hence, as a banker's Credit produces him exactly the same Profit as Money would: it is evident that his Credit is Capital to him just as much as Money is

Again, Credits, Debts, or Rights of action, are Goods, Chattels, Commodities, Merchandise

Now, under the term Circulating Capital, Smith expressly includes the Goods or Commodities in shops. The trader buys the goods at a lower price from one person, and sells them at a higher price to other persons : and so makes a profit by them : and thus the goods in the shop are **Capital** to him

So a banker buys the Goods, Commodities, or Merchandise termed Debts at a lower price from one person, his own customer, and sells them at a higher price to another, namely, the Acceptor, or Debtor. The debt the banker buys is increasing in value every day, from the time he buys it until it is paid off. These goods, commodities, or commodities termed Debts in the portfolio of the banker, produce him a profit just in the same way as the goods, commodities, or merchandise in the shop produce profits to the trader

Hence the Bills in the portfolio of a banker are **Circulating Capital** exactly in the same way as the goods, commodities, or merchandise in the shop of a trader are **Circulating Capital**

On the **Caution** *necessary in applying* **Mathematics** *to* **Economics**

14. We now see how necessary caution is in applying Mathematics to Economics : and how indispensable it is to have a precise and accurate statement of facts so that the Mathematics may be subservient to the facts : and not the mistress of them

Several distinguished Algebraists, in acknowledging that Debts are Negative Quantities, put it in this way—" If property possessed or due could be denoted by a number or symbol with a Positive sign, a Debt would be denoted by a number or symbol with a Negative sign : or conversely. Such affections of Property (?) are correctly symbolised by the signs + and — : since they possess the inverse relations to each other which these signs require : for if to a person A there be given a certain property or sum of money, combined with or added to a Debt of equal amount, his Wealth or Property remains the same as before "

We have already several times pointed out that Algebraists are in error in applying the signs + and — in Economics to property : they do not affect **Property** but **Persons**

The mode of statement adopted by these Algebraists has a plausible appearance : and in a certain sense may be correct. If a person were going to retire from business, he would call in and discharge his liabilities : and the remainder, if any, would be his fortune

It may also be conceded that if a person acquires a sum of money, and at the same time is charged with an equal amount of Debt, he is no richer than he was before. But such a mode of statement is quite unsuitable for Economics, as is shown most clearly when applied to Banking. Because when a banker buys £10,000 in cash from his customers, he is exactly in the position described by these Algebraists. He has brought £10,000 in cash from his customers by creating an exactly equal amount of Debts, or Rights of action, against himself. His property is therefore correctly stated as £10,000 — £10,000 : and, therefore, no doubt, he is substantially in exactly the same position as he was before : *he* is neither the richer nor the poorer

But that is an extremely erroneous view to take of the matter as regards the science of Economics. Economics has only to do with the number of Economic Quantities in actual existence at any given instant, and with their exchangeable relations

Now, when a banker acquires £10,000 in cash from his customers they receive in exchange an equal sum in Rights of action which are their property. Thus by this operation there has been created a new Property, which may circulate in commerce, and effect exchanges or payments exactly like an equal sum of money

No doubt these Rights of action may be extinguished. They were created by one exchange and they may be extinguished by another exchange. But so long as they remain in existence they are Economic Quantities, like any others. The £10,000 in cash remain the absolute property of the banker, which he may trade with in any way he pleases : and he has only the abstract personal Duty to buy up these Rights of action, if required to do so. The Negative sign in no way affects his material Property ; but only his Person : and it has no effect whatever until he is called upon to buy up the Rights of action against himself

To show the subtle nature of the question, let us again consider the accounts between a banker and his customers. From the banker's point of view his assets, whether Cash or Bills, are his absolute Property, (+) : and his liabilities are his Debts, or his personal duty to pay, (—) : and his accounts would be stated thus—

LIABILITIES.—			ASSETS.+		
Deposits	.. ..	£49,600	Cash		£10,000
			Bills of Exchange ..		40,000
		£49,600			£50,000

But, from the customers' point of view the case is exactly reversed. The banker's liabilities are the absolute property of his customers, (+) : and the banker's Duty is to meet these claims out of his Assets, (—). Hence, from the customers' point of view, the accounts would stand thus—

RIGHTS OF ACTION					BANKER'S ASSETS				
	+					—			
Deposits ..	..	..	£49,600	Cash ..	..	..	..	£10,600
				Bills ..	..	..	..	40,000
			———					———
			£49,600					£50,000
				Balance + ..	..	..	400

The balance of £400 is evidently the banker's own property

Hence, generally, the accounts between a banker and his customers may be stated thus—

Deposits		—					+			
		+					—			
Deposits	..	..	£49,600	Cash ..	..	..	..	£10,600
				Bills ..	..	..	..	40,000
			———					———
			£49,600					£50,000
				Balance	..	..	..	400

where the upper or lower signs are to be taken according as they are regarded from the banker's or the customers' point of view

The fact is that every Obligation bears the double sign $\pm$: and these opposite signs do not cancel each other, as many writers suppose : but the Right of action is a saleable and exchangeable Quantity as long as it exists : and until it is paid off and extinguished : and the Negative sign denotes the personal Duty of the Debtor to pay when required to do so : but it in no way affects any property he may have so as to give his Creditors any claim or right to it

On the Clearing House

15. One of the great improvements in modern times in the organisation of Credit is the institution of Clearing Houses : and as the effect of these, like everything else in Banking, is the subject of great misconception, we must explain their operation

It is usually supposed that the Clearing House is an example of the principle of Compensation, like that effected by the foreign merchants at the Continental fairs. In foreign treatises the Clearing House is usually called a *Maison de Compensation* or *de Liquidation*. This, however, is a complete error

It has been shown that if any number of customers of the same bank have transactions among themselves, and give each other cheques on their accounts, any number of transactions may be settled by Transfers of Credits from one account to another without a single coin being required, so long as the receiver of the Cheque does not draw out the money

Such a Transfer is a *Novatio*

The Clearing system is a device by which all the Banks which join in it are formed, as it were, into one huge banking institution, for the purpose of transferring Credits from one bank to another without the use of coin; just in the same way as Credits are transferred in the same bank from one account to another, without the use of coin

The Clearing House, therefore, is not a *Maison de Liquidation* or of *Compensation*, but it is a *Maison de Novations*

Every banker has every morning claims on behalf of his customers against his neighbours, and they have claims on behalf of their customers against him. These claims are called bankers' charges. Formerly it was the custom for every banker to send out his clerks the first thing in the morning to collect these charges, which had to be paid in money or bank notes. Having collected these charges, he credited his customers with the sums due to them

But each of his neighbours had also claims on behalf of their customers against him. Consequently every banker was obliged to keep a large amount of money and bank notes to meet these claims. By this means a very large amount of money and notes had to be retained for the sole purpose of meeting these bankers' charges, which could be made no other use of

It was stated in evidence before the House of Commons many years ago, that one bank alone, the London and Westminster, was obliged to keep £150,000 in notes for this sole purpose. And if one bank alone, then comparatively in its infancy, was obliged to keep such a sum idle for this purpose, what would have been the sum necessary to be retained at the present day by all the banks, if it were not for the Clearing House?

To remedy this inconvenience an ingenious plan was devised, it is said by the banks at Naples in the sixteenth century. The Banks instituted a central chamber to which each sent a clerk. These clerks exchanged their different claims against each other, and paid only the difference in money

By this means the different Credits were readjusted among the different customers' accounts just as easily as before: and an immense amount of money and notes were set free for the purpose of circulation and commerce: and were, in fact, for all practical purposes, equivalent to so much increase of Capital to the banks and to the country

This system was first adopted in this country by the Banks in Edinburgh. And we have now to show that no destruction or annihilation of Credit takes place as in Compensation: but only a **Transfer** of Credit, that is a *Novation*

Suppose that a customer of the Commercial Bank has £100 in notes of the Royal Bank paid to him. He is then Creditor of the Royal Bank. He pays these notes into his account with the Commercial Bank; and thus constitutes them his agents to collect the notes from the Royal Bank, and place the proceeds to his credit

Suppose that in a similar way a customer of the Royal Bank has £100 in notes of the Commercial Bank paid to him

Then he is Creditor of the Commercial Bank. He pays these notes into his account with the Royal Bank: and so constitutes them his agents to collect the proceeds and place them to his credit

Each bank is then Debtor to the customer of the other

The full way of proceeding then would be for each bank to send a clerk to the other to collect the notes in money. Each bank, then, having obtained payment of the notes in money would place that sum to the credit of its customer, and put the money into its own till, which would become its property, just as if its customer had paid in the money himself

In this case it is evident that there is no annihilation or extinction of Credit: because by the process each Bank, instead of being debtor to the customer of the other, becomes debtor to its own customer

Thus it is evident that in each case there is a *Novation*: and not a *Compensation*

This method of settling the claims of the customers of the banks would require £200 in money

The same result may be attained in a much simpler way

Let the agents of the two Banks meet. The agent of the Commercial Bank says to the agent of the Royal Bank—" In consideration of your giving up to me the notes held by your customer by which I am debtor to him, and so releasing me from my debt to him, I agree to credit my customer with their amount "

The agent of the Royal Bank says to the agent of the Commercial Bank—" In consideration of your giving up to me the notes held by your customer by which I am debtor to him, and so releasing me from my debt to him, I agree to credit my customer with their amount, and so become debtor to him "

The agents of the two banks then exchange notes: and each bank having received £100 in its own notes—that is, being released from its debt to the customer of the other, which, as we have seen is equivalent to a payment in money—enters the amount to the credit of its own customer

By this means each bank, instead of being debtor to the customer of the other, becomes debtor to its own customer : and the use of £200 in money is saved

No doubt the £100 of notes of each bank is withdrawn from circulation and replaced in its own till. But an equal amount of Credit is placed to the credit of each customer. So that the quantity of Credit remains exactly the same

Thus, the debt of each bank to the customer of the other is extinguished by the new debt created in favor of its own customer

Thus, the whole transaction consists of two *Novations*

The reason why the operations of the merchants at the continental fairs were Compensations in which both Credits were extinguished: and the operations of the Clearing house are Novations in which merely new Credits are created, which extinguished the old ones, but create an equal amount of new credits, so that the whole amount of Credit remains exactly the same, is this—

In the case of the merchants they were principals : and they were mutually indebted to each other : when, therefore, they exchanged their debts they were cancelled and extinguished, and no new debt was created to replace them

But in the case of the Clearing House the banks are not principals ; they are only agents for their customers : consequently when they receive their own notes, and so are released from their debts to the customer of the other, they are bound to create an equal amount of credit in favor of their customers, which cancels and extinguishes the former debt, but leaves exactly the same amount of credit existing

Hence the Clearing House is a *Maison de Novation :* and not of *Liquidation* or *Compensation*

The system of clearing was adopted by the City bankers in 1776, but the Bank of England was not admitted to it. Nor were the Joint Stock Banks admitted to it till 1854, when the charges of the Joint Stock Banks pressed so heavily on the private bankers that they were obliged to admit them. The Bank of England was not admitted till 1864

The charges of the London bankers consist in cheques and not in notes : but that makes no difference in the principles of the case. They collect the cheques due to their customers, and rearrange the credits to the various parties exactly in the same way as if they were notes

Before 1864 the differences payable by the banks were settled by notes, and it is said that about £250,000 were required for that purpose

But in 1864, when the Bank of England was admitted the system of clearing was further improved : so that the use of coin and bank notes was entirely dispensed with. Every clearing bank keeps an account with the Bank of England : and the Inspector of the Clearing House keeps one also. Printed lists of the clearing banks are made out for each bank with its own name at the top : and the others placed in alphabetical order below it. On the left side is the Debtor's column, and on the right the Creditor's. The clerk of the Clearing House then makes up the accounts between each bank, and the difference only is entered in the balance sheet according as it is Debtor or Creditor. A balance is then struck between the Debtor and Creditor side, and the paper delivered to the clerk who takes it back to his own bank. The balance is then paid to or received from the Clearing House. If the bank is debtor it gives a white ticket to, and when it is creditor it receives a green ticket from the Clearing House. By this system not a single coin or bank note is used : and the sum transferred by this means, exceeds £6,000,000,000 a year

On the Transformation of Temporary Credit into Permanent Capital

16. We shall now give an example of the doctrine that the **Release of a Debt** is in all cases equivalent to a **Payment in Money**, which may surprise some of our readers, and of which we have not seen the slightest notice anywhere else

When it is published to the world that the Bank of England has a paid up Capital of £14,000,000 : and that the several Joint-Stock Banks have paid up Capitals of some millions, most persons take it for granted that these Banks have these sums paid up in hard cash

Nevertheless, this is a profound error. Of course it is impossible for any stranger to have a precise knowledge as to how much of these amounts was ever paid up in actual money. But it may probably be said with safety that not so much as half of these various amounts was ever paid up in real money : and that at least one-half of these various amounts of "Capital" was never anything more than the Bank's own **Credit** turned into **Capital**

To explain this we may observe that the first subscription to the Bank of England was £1,200,000, paid, of course, in actual money. It was advanced to Government, and the Bank was allowed to issue an equal amount in Notes

In 1696 the Bank stopped payment, and its Notes fell to a discount of 20 per cent.

In 1697 Parliament undertook the restoration of public credit : and it was determined to increase the Capital of the Bank by £1,000,000 : but not one penny of this was paid up in actual money

The Act directed that £800,000 of the subscription should be paid up in Exchequer Tallies, or Exchequer Bills : and the remaining £200,000 in the Bank's own depreciated Notes : which were received at their full par value in cash

Thus of its first increase of Capital £200,000 consisted of its own depreciated Notes.   The Bank was authorised to issue an additional amount of Notes equal to its increase of Capital.   At subsequent increases of Capital the subscribers might pay up any amount they pleased in the Bank's own Notes, which were considered as equivalent to a payment in Money : and an increase of Capital

In 1727 the Bank of Scotland increased its Capital.   The subscription was paid up partly in the Bank's own Notes.   An outcry was made against this.   But the Directors justly answered— "But the objectors do not at all consider this point, for the payments are many of them made in specie : and Bank Notes are justly reckoned the same as specie, when paid in on a call of stock, because, when paid in, *it lessens the demand on the Bank*"

Hence, the Directors clearly understood that the *Release of a Debt* is in all respects equivalent to a *Payment in Money*

The Bank had issued its Notes, and were, of course, Debtors to the holders of them.   These Debts were Negative Quantities : the subscribers might either pay in money, which was $+ \times +$: or Release the Bank from its Debts, which was $- \times -$: and the effect of either transaction was exactly the same.   At every increase of Capital the very same operations would be repeated : payment in Money and in the Bank's own Notes would always be treated as equivalent.   And hence, at every fresh increase of Capital, a certain amount of the Bank's own **Temporary Credit** was turned into **Permanent Capital**

Thus we see that the Parliament of England and the Directors of the Bank of Scotland, who were probably equally innocent of

Algebra and Roman Law, simply from their own mercantile instinct, treated the Release of a Debt as in all respects equivalent to a Payment in Money

Banks, therefore, which issue Notes may increase their Capital by receiving their own Notes in payment : by which they turn their own Credit into Capital. But Banks which do not issue Notes may increase their Capital exactly in the same way. A customer of the Bank who has a balance at his Credit is in exactly the same position as a Note holder. If he wishes to subscribe to an increase of Capital he simply gives the Bank a Cheque on his account. This is equally a Release from a Debt as a payment in the Bank's own Notes, and an increase of Capital

If the customer has not sufficient on his account to pay for the stock he wishes to buy he may bring the Bank bills to discount. The Bank discounts those bills by creating a Credit or Deposit in his favor, which, of course, is a Negative Quantity, exactly like a Bank Note. The customer then gives the Bank a Cheque on his account—that is, he Releases the Bank from the Debt it has created : and that Debt released becomes increase of Capital

This is the way in which the Capital of all Joint-Stock Banks is increased : and it may go on to any extent without any payment in Money. And, consequently, it is wholly impossible for any person, who has not had access to the books of the Bank, to ascertain what proportion of the Capital consists of payments in Money, and what proportion consists of the Bank's own **Temporary Credit** turned into **Permanent Capital**

On the Scotch System of Banking

17. The Credits, or Rights of action, created by Bankers in the operations we have been describing, were employed to buy Commercial Bills which arose out of the **Transfer** of commodities : and it has been shown that they create Credit to several times the amount of their Cash in possession. And some writers suppose that this is the limit of legitimate Credit. It is very commonly imagined that Credit can only be used to transfer existing commodities

We have now to describe a species of Credit of a totally different nature, invented in Scotland, to which the marvelous progress of that country is mainly due

It is Credit created, not for the purpose of transferring or circulating commodities already to existence, but for the express purpose of calling **New Products** into existence. It is entirely of the nature of **Accommodation Paper** : and it will show that there is nothing in the nature of Accommodation Paper more dangerous or objectionable than Real Paper—as it is called : but, on the contrary, they stand exactly on the same footing of security : and also that Credit is equally applicable to call **new** products into existence as to transfer those already in existence

When, after a long period of inactivity, the energies of a people are suddenly turned into an industrial direction, they find innumerable enterprises which would be profitable if only they possessed the means of setting them agoing. The quantity of money which was sufficient for a non-industrial people is now found to be wholly inadequate for the increased demand for it : and the only consequence can be, that if there is a greatly increased demand for the existing quantity of money the rate of Interest will rise enormously : and to such an extent as to preclude all possibility of profit from such enterprises even if effected

It is, therefore, invariably found that whenever this takes place multitudes of schemes are set afloat for increasing the quantity of money

For many centuries after the Conquest, England was essentially a feudal and military—an agricultural and pastoral people. Its Law was almost entirely feudal and related to the tenure of Land. Merchants and commerce were held in very subordinate esteem, and Commercial Law had no existence. In the sixteenth century the energies of the nation were absorbed in religious controversies : and in the first half of the next century in constitutional struggles and politics. At length, in the reign of Charles II., men, weary of polemics and politics, began to devote themselves more to industry and commerce : and this was greatly stimulated by the manifest advantages of Banking, which had just been introduced into England

Among fields of enterprise at that period none seemed more promising than agriculture. But, unfortunately, all the available specie was absorbed in commerce: none was to be had for agriculture: or, at least, only at such rates as to be practically prohibitory

In no species of industry are the profits so moderate as in agriculture. Hence, if Capital has to be borrowed to effect improvements in agriculture, it is requisite that it should be at a very low rate of interest. The usual rate of interest, in the time of Charles II., was 10 per cent., and few improvements in agriculture could bear that. But, by the introduction of Banking, and the foundation of the Bank of England, the rate of interest in commerce had been reduced to 3 per cent.

It was this real want and the enormous advantage which Banking had been to commerce, which gave rise to the schemes of Asgill, Briscoe, Chamberlen, Law, and others, for the purpose of turning the Land into Money; and to found Land Banks to assist agriculture, as the Mercantile Banks had assisted Commerce, which were so rife at this period

One of these schemes was attempted to be carried out in 1696. The ministry of William III. was not, as is now the case, formed exclusively of one party in the state. William III. reigned and governed, and the ministry was his ministry, and not that of the Parliament, as it is now. His ministry was partly Whig and partly Tory. The Whig portion of it, who were in close connection with the mercantile community of the city, succeeded in founding the Bank of England in 1694: which was essentially a Whig project, and intended to assist the finance of the Government and commerce

The immense benefit of the Bank of England was so evident that the Tory portion of the ministry endeavored to found a Bank which should also assist Goverment, and also be specially for the benefit of agriculture. It was attempted to be founded in 1696: and it was called the Land Bank. But the attempt did not succeed: and its failure was one of the causes which produced the stoppage of the Bank of England in 1697. There were, no doubt, defects in the scheme which fully accounted for its failure: but the want was very real: and the idea was perfectly sound

Among the projectors of a scheme for basing Paper Money on land the most celebrated was John Law. He has given an elaborate exposition of his theory in a work termed *Money and Trade Considered;* and he laid a scheme before the Parliament of Scotland in 1705, which they fortunately rejected, or there would have been a catastrophe as great as that of the Darien Scheme in 1699. Law had the opportunity of reducing his theory to practice in France, in 1720, under the name of the Mississippi Scheme

This is not the place to give an account of Law's scheme which we have done elsewhere.[1] But ten years after its failure in France, the Scotch Banks, by the admirable invention of Cash Credits, pushed Credit to the utmost extent of its legitimate limits, and realised all that was practicable in the schemes of Asgill, Briscoe, Chamberlen, and Law. And it is to these Cash Credits that the principal progress of Scotland in agriculture and all public works is due, as well as the personal wealth of its merchants

Moreover, after the end of the Seven Years' War in 1763 an ingenious merchant devised a scheme of Land Banks in Germany: and it is to these Land Banks that the principal part of the progress of agriculture in central Europe is due

On Cash Credits

18. The Bank of Scotland was founded in 1695 with unlimited powers of issue, both in amount and denomination. At first it only issued Notes of £100, £50, £10, and £5. Though several times advised to do so, they did not issue £1 Notes : but in 1704 they began to do so. The Bank received a monopoly of banking for 21 years : but in 1727, when the monopoly expired and they endeavoured to have it renewed, there was such a strenuous outburst of public feeling against it that they did not succeed

In that year the proprietors of the Equivalent Fund were endowed by Royal Charter with powers of banking : and they assumed the name of the Royal Bank

In the very contracted sphere of commerce in Scotland at that time, there were not sufficient Commercial Bills in circulation to

---

[1] *Dictionary of Political Economy.* Art. " Banking in France "

exhaust the Credit of the Banks. They had, as it were, a superfluity of unexhausted Credit on hand : and the new Bank devised a new scheme for getting its Credit into circulation which was the most marvelous development of Credit ever imagined

It agreed on receiving sufficient guarantees to open Credits to certain limited amounts in favor of trustworthy and respectable persons

A Cash Credit is, therefore, a Drawing Account created in favor of a person who pays in no money, which he may operate upon precisely in the same manner as on an ordinary account : the only difference being that instead of receiving interest on the daily balance at his credit, as was formerly the case in Scotland, he is charged interest on the daily balance at his Debit. A Cash Credit is, therefore, an **Inverse** drawing account

Cash Credits are applicable to a totally different class of transactions to those which give rise to Bills of Exchange. One difference being that Bills of Exchange arise out of the transfers of commodities, and are payable in one sum at a fixed date. Whereas Cash Credits are not issued on the transfer of commodities : or on any previous transactions. They are not repayable at any fixed date : but they are a continuous working account which continues open as long as the operations are satisfactory

It is a condition of all Cash Credits that the persons to whom they are granted should accept all advances in the Bank's own Notes

In order to understand clearly the principles of the system, it is only necessary to recur to our fundamental definition or Concept of Credit. Because a true fundamental definition or Concept is the polestar to guide us through all difficulties and perplexities. " There is nothing in the world," said the Duke of Wellington, with his commanding common sense, " like a good Definition "

It has been shown in the preceding chapters that the true definition of **Credit** is the " **Present Right** or the **Present Value** of a **Future Profit**." And every **Future Profit**, from whatever source arising, or of whatsoever nature, has a **Present Value**, which may be recorded on any material, such as paper, and may be brought into commerce, and may be bought and sold and transferred by manual delivery, exactly like money or any other material chattel

It has been shown that Land is an Economic Quantity which produces a continuous series of Profits: and that a trader exercising any profitable business is an Economic Quantity analogous to land, and produces a continuous series of profits

We have explained the complete system of Mercantile Credit: and shown that its true limits are the future profits of Mercantile traders. That all Credit is sound which is redeemed at maturity: and that Mercantile Banking consists in buying up the rights to be paid out of these future profits of mercantile traders

Now, having argued from the Land to Commerce, let us reverse the case, and argue from Commerce to the Land

If every future Commercial Profit has a Present Value, which can be brought into commerce and exchanged, the same is equally true of the Land and every commercial public work or enterprise. The Present Value of every future profit from Land or any commercial work can be brought into commerce and bought and sold exactly like the Present Value of the Future Profits of mercantile persons. And if the Credit be strictly limited and redeemed by the future profits of the land or commercial public work, Credit may be created to purchase the Present Values of these Future Profits from Land and commercial public works exactly in the same way as it is created to purchase the Present Values of the Future Profits from mercantile traders

Cash Credits are applied in two different ways—

1. To aid private persons in business
2. To promote agriculture and the formation of commercial works of all kinds

Cash Credits granted in aid of persons

19. Every man in business, however humble, or however extensive, must necessarily keep a certain portion of ready money by him, to answer immediate demands for small daily expenses, wages, and other things. This could, of course, be much more profitably employed in his business, where it might produce a profit of fifteen or twenty per cent., instead of lying idle. But unless the trader knew that he could command it at a moment's notice, he would always be obliged to keep a certain amount of ready money in his own till, unless he is able to command the use of some one else's till

Now one object of a Cash Credit is to supply this convenience to the trader, and to enable him to invest the whole of his capital in his business : and upon proper security being given to furnish him with the accommodation of a till at a moment's notice, in such small sums as he may require, on his paying a moderate interest for the accommodation

Almost every trader in Scotland has a Cash Credit at a Bank, by which he can draw out such sums as he may want for his daily business, and replace such as he does not want before the close of bank hours

Almost every young man commencing business in Scotland does it by means of a Cash Credit. Thus, for instance, lawyers, or writers to the signet, commencing business, have occasion for ready money from day to day, before they can get in payments from their clients. It is a great bar to any young man to commence the business of a solicitor without Capital, which must either be his own, or furnished to him by his friends. It is an immense advantage to him, and to them, to have it supplied by a Bank, by means of a Cash Credit, on a mere guarantee, a mere contingency which they never would give if they thought there was any danger of its being enforced

So, the great employers of labor, manufacturers, builders, ship builders, and all others, have Cash Credits, by which they can pay their laborers

These Credits are granted to all classes of society : to the poor as freely as to the rich. Everything depends upon **Character.** Young men in the humblest walks of life may inspire their friends with confidence in their steadiness and judgment and they become sureties for them on a Cash Credit. This is in all respects of equal value to them as money : and thus, they have the means placed within their reach of rising to any extent that their abilities and industry permit them, Multitudes of men who have raised themselves to immense wealth began life with nothing but a Cash Credit. As one example among thousands, Mr. Menteith, M.P., told the Committee of the House of Commons, in 1826, that he was a manufacturer, employing at that time 4,000 hands : and that, except with the merest trifle of Capital lent to him, and which he very soon paid off, he began the world with nothing but a Cash Credit !

The Banks usually limit their advances to a certain moderate amount, varying from £100 to £1,000 in general : and they always take several sureties in each case : never less than two, and sometimes many more. These cautioners, as they are termed in Scotch Law, keep a watchful eye on the proceedings of the customer, and have always the right of inspecting his account with the bank, and of stopping it at any time, if irregular. These Credits are not meant to degenerate into dead loans, but they are required to be constantly operated upon, by paying in and drawing out

The enormous amount of transactions carried on by this kind of account may be judged of by the evidence given before the Committee of the Commons, in 1826. It was then stated that on a Credit of £1,000 operations to the extent of £50,000 took place in a single week. Its effects, therefore, were exactly the same as if there had been 1,000 sovereigns. Others stated that on a Cash Credit of £500 operations to the amout of £70,000 took place in a year. One witness stated that in a very moderately-sized country bank, operations to the amount of £90,000,000 took place in twenty-one years : and that the whole loss to the bank during that time was £1,200

At that time it was conjectured that there were about 12,000 Cash Credits guaranteed by about 40,000 sureties, who were interested in the integrity, prudence, and success of the others. The witnesses before the Lords declared that the effects of these were most remarkable on the morals of the people

On **Cash Credits** *granted to promote* **Agriculture,** *and the*
Formation of Public Works

20. We have now to consider the way in which the Scotch
System of Cash Credits has been applied to promote Agriculture,
and the formation of all manner of Public Works

In the first chapter, we explained the Theory of the Value of
Land, and showed that a successful trader is an Economic
Quantity analogous to land ; inasmuch as he produces a continuous
series of Profits

We have shown that all Mercantile Banking consists in discounting or buying the Rights to be paid out of the future profits
of traders

Now having argued from the Land to Persons, let us reverse
the case, and argue from **Persons** to the **Land**

If Mercantile Banks can be founded for the purpose of
discounting the future profits of Traders, Banks may also be
founded to discount the future profits of the Land

The only two Scotch Banks which existed at first, applied their
Cash Credits to assist the industry of traders, and tended much to
foster it.   But agricultural industry had not awoke.   The Scotch
were a fierce, turbulent people, who thought a great deal more
of harrying their neighbours, and raiding their cattle, than of
peaceful agriculture.   The land was bound down under the fetters
of the feudal system.   But after the suppression of the rising in
1746, the feudal system was to a great extent broken up, and a
great spirit of enterprise awoke, and then for the first time Scotland
became an industrial nation

At this time there were, in many parts of Scotland, large
tracts of reclaimable land and multitudes of people, but they
remained unemployed, because there was no Money in the country
to set their industry in motion

Now suppose that a proprietor of one of these tracts of land
had had £10,000 in money : and that he had employed it in
paying wages to laborers, and in buying seed to sow : then, in
course of time, the value of the produce of the land would replace

the sum expended in bringing the land into cultivation with a profit. Then the money so employed would have been expended as **Capital**

But, at that time, there was, comparatively speaking, no money in the country. But the Banks having habituated the people, during the course of about 40 years, to receive their £1 Notes in all respects as money, and, having acquired their thorough confidence, threw out branches in all directions, and sent down boxes of their £1 Notes

Farmers, at that time, had no votes in Scotland : and consequently the landlords had no motives to keep their tenants in political subjection : as was too much the case in England. They adopted every means possible to develope the resources of the soil. And, as it was not to be expected that the farmers should lay out their capital and industry on the soil without security of tenure, it became the custom almost universal in Scotland for landlords to grant their tenants leases of 19 years : and, in many cases, much longer than that

Upon the security of these leases, and also upon that of personal friends, the Banks everywhere granted Cash Credits to the farmers : the advances being made exclusively in their own £1 Notes. From the strong constitution of the Banks, and the universal confidence they had acquired, their Notes were universally received as Cash : and, though they were demandable in cash at the Head Office, no one ever dreamt of demanding payment for them

With these advances in £1 Notes the farmers employed the laborers in reclaiming the land, and sowed the crops. The Notes were employed in exactly the same way as Money would have been, and they produced exactly the same effects as Money would have done. The land was reclaimed, and sown, and stocked : and, in a few years, bleak and barren moors were everywhere changed into fields of waving corn : and they produced a continuous series of profits. With the value of the produce the farmers gradually repaid the loans, and reaped a profit

Now if it be admitted that Money expended in agricultural improvements is used as Productive Capital; how can it be denied that Credit employed in exactly the same way, and which produces exactly the same effects in every way as Money, and produces exactly the same profits, is also equally **Productive Capital ?**

The £1 Notes were universally received by the people as of exactly the same value as Money : and, therefore, they were in all respects Money : and they produced exactly the same profits that money did. Now as we have seen that Capital is Anything which produces a profit : it is evident that the £1 notes were just as much **Productive Capital** as the Money

The only difference was that in using Money, the employer made Capital of the **realised** Profits of the **Past** : in using Credit, he made Capital of the **expected** Profits of the **Future.** But the results were exactly the same in either case

Every one acquainted with Scotland knows perfectly well that the prodigious progress in agriculture made in that country during the last 130 years has been almost entirely effected by means of these Cash Credits

Not only has almost the entire progress in agriculture been effected by these Cash Credits, but all public works of every description—Roads, Canals, Docks, Harbours, Railways, Public Buildings, &c., have also been made by means of Cash Credits

It was stated to the Committee of the House of Commons in 1826, that the Forth and Clyde Canal was executed by means of a Cash Credit of £40,000, granted by the Royal Bank. So when a Road has to be made, the Trustees obtain a Cash Credit, and pay it off out of the rates. So when a Railway, a Dock, a Harbour, a Public Building is to be erected, the Directors obtain a Cash Credit, and so pay the wages of the men. We have already, in the preceding chapter, given the instance of the Market at Guernsey, being built by Notes issued by the States, secured on the future profits of the Market. The great Cash Credit system of the Scotch Banks is absolutely the same thing, only on a prodigiously enlarged and more organised system

It is thus seen how Credit is applied to the **Formation** of **New** products equally well as to the **Transfer** of existing ones. Credit is Purchasing Power equally as Money : and it may be applied to the purchase of **Labor** to form **New** products, equally well as to Transfer existing ones. The principle of the Limit, however, being exactly the same in both cases : namely, that it is the **Present Value** of the **Future Profit**

When Money is used to produce a profit, it is expected that the profit shall replace the money advanced : when Credit is used to produce a profit, it is expected that the profit shall redeem the Debt incurred

Hence Credit can do whatever Money can do : but we have shown that Credit is the inverse of Money. Hence, in Mathematical language, all the propositions which are true with respect to Money are equally true with respect to Credit : only with the sign changed

Exactly the same effects were produced in England by the use of Bankers' Notes. The success of the Bridgewater Canal had exactly a similar effect as the success of the Liverpool and Manchester Railway. The period from 1776 to 1796 was just as great an era in Canal Making as the subsequent period in Railway Building. In the course of 20 years England, from being the most backward country in Europe in water communication, was covered with a network of canals such as no other country but Holland can boast. These canals were made by bankers' notes. Burke says that when he first came to England there were not twelve bankers out of London. In 1793 there were 400. However, these bankers, not having the solid constitution of the Scotch Banks, were swept away in multitudes in the panic of 1793. But, nevertheless, though the bankers were swept away, the solid results of their issues of notes remained

Thus it is now clearly demonstrated that **Credit** may be used as **Productive Capital**, exactly in the same way and in the same sense, and for all the purposes, that money is

Remarks on the Scotch System of Cash Credits

21. All these marvelous results which have raised Scotland from the lowest depths of barbarism up to her present proud position in the space of 170 years, are the children of pure Credit. It is no exaggeration but a melancholy truth, that at the period of the Revolution in 1688, and the foundation of the

Bank of Scotland in 1695, that country, partly owing to such a series of disasters as cannot be paralleled in the history of any other independent nation : and partly owing to its position in the very outskirts of civilisation, and far removed from the humanising influences of commerce : divided into two nations, aliens in blood and language : was the most utterly lawless and barbarous country in Europe.   And it is equally undeniable that the two great causes of her rapid rise in civilisation and wealth have been her systems of National Education and Banking

Her system of Banking has been of infinitely greater service to her than mines of gold and silver.   Mines of the precious metals would probably have only demoralised the people, and made them more savage than even they were before.   But her Banking system has tended immensely to call forth every manly virtue. It has taught them industry, steadiness, and moral rectitude. In the **Character** of her own people, Scotland has found **Wealth** infinitely more beneficial to her than all the mines of Mexico and Peru

The express purpose of the Banks was to create **Credits**, Incorporeal entities, created out of **Nothing**, for a transitory existence : and when they had performed their functions vanishing again into the **Nothing** from whence they sprang.   And has not this **Credit** been **Capital**?   Will any one with these results staring the world in the face, believe that there are still some persons who are supposed to be Economists, who maintain that the results of Credit are purely imaginary !   That Credit conduces nothing to Production and the increase of Wealth !   That Credit only transfers existing Capital.   But even if it did no more than that, it has been shown that *Circulation* or **Transfer** is one species of Production : as is indeed admitted by all Economists.   And that those persons who say that Credit is Capital are such puzzle headed dolts, as to maintain that the same thing can be in two places at once !

The fact is that Circulating Credits of all kinds have exactly the same effect as Money, both in circulating existing commodities, and in promoting the formation of new products.   And they may be used as Productive Capital in the same method and in the same sense that Money is

Now it must be observed that all these Cash Credits are for a distinct purpose, quite different from the discount of Mercantile Paper. The marvelous results they have produced are due to a system of pure **Accommodation Paper**. They are not founded upon any previous transactions : nor are they for the purpose of transferring existing commodities. They are created for the express purpose of forming **New** products, which, but for them, would either have had no existence at all : or at all events would have been deferred for a very long period, until solid money could have been accumulated to effect them. They are founded on exactly the same principles as the discount of Mercantile Bills. In discounting Mercantile Bills the banker merely buys up the Right to a future payment to be made out of the profits of the transaction. In creating Cash Credits the Banker merely buys the Right to a future payment to be made out of the future profits of the land or other public works

The invention of Cash Credits has advanced the Wealth of Scotland by centuries. We have an enormous mass of Exchangeable Property created out of Nothing by the mere will of the Bank and its customers, which produces all the effects of solid gold and silver : and when it has done its work, it vanishes again into Nothing, at the will of the same persons who called it into existence. Hence we see that the mere will of man has created vast masses of **Wealth** out of **Nothing** : and then having served their purpose, they were **Decreated** into **Nothing** : which are—

"Melted into air, into thin air"

But their solid results have by no means faded

"Like the baseless fabric of a vision
Leaving not a wreck behind"

On the contrary, their solid results have been vast tracts of barren moor converted into fields of waving corn : the manufactures of Glasgow, Dundee, and Paisley : the unrivaled steam ships of the Clyde : great public works of all sorts : roads : canals : bridges : harbours : docks : railroads : and poor young men raised up into princely merchants

What the Nile is to Egypt that has her Banking system been to Scotland : and it was fortunate for her that the foundations of her prosperity were laid broad and deep before the gigantic fallacy was dreamt of that the Issues of Banks should be inexorably restricted to the amount of gold they displace : that no increase of money can be of any use to a country : and before Mill had proclaimed to the world that to create Credit in excess of specie is robbery !

The reader will now perceive the gigantic utility of the £1 note system to Scotland : and the consternation and fury of the Scotch people when various attempts have been made by Parliament to suppress them. When Parliament suppressed £1 Notes in England in consequence of the evils they produced, owing to the bad organisation of the English Banking system, before the monopoly of the Bank of England was first broken up in 1826, it was intended to have suppressed them also in Scotland. But all Scotland rose up against it : and, headed by Malachi Malagrowther, raised such a commotion that an inquiry was granted, which first made the Scotch System of Banking understood, and the attempt was abandoned. Still, however, constant jeers and gibes were addressed to the Scotch, by persons who knew nothing about the subject, about their fatuous attachment to their dirty £1 Notes. But the Scotch knew their value to the country far better than their assailants. The Scotch knew by experience that the prosperity of their country was bound up with Cash Credits : and Cash Credits were bound up with the issue of £1 Notes. To have suppressed the Scotch £1 Notes at that time would have destroyed two-thirds of the business of the Banks. The extent of Commerce in Scotland at that time was not sufficient to support the great Banks. We have been informed that at that time two-thirds of the business of the Scotch Banks consisted in Cash Credits : though whether it continues to be so still we cannot say

Happily, however, no such attempts will ever be made again, now that the subject is better understood. But Parliament is, however, justified in taking any measures it may be deemed necessary to secure their perfect safety and convertibility. So completely has the tide of opinion changed that the question now is whether £1 Notes can be re-introduced into England. But with the present transitional state of Banking in England, that is far too complicated and profound a subject to be entered upon here

On the **Land Banks** of *Germany :* or **Banks** of **Credit Foncier**

23. At the close of the Seven Years' War in 1763, the proprietors in Silesia found themselves in a state of inextricable embarrassment. The ruin and destruction caused by the war, and the low price of corn caused by the general distress, made them unable to meet their engagements. Interest and commission rose to 13 per cent. They obtained a respite of three years to pay their debts. To alleviate the distress arising out of this state of matters, a Berlin merchant named Büring invented a system of Land Credit which has been very extensively adopted in Germany, Russia, Poland, and lastly in France

Proprietors of land can no doubt borrow money on mortgage : but in every country such transactions are attended with many inconveniences. They have many expensive formalities to undergo, such as investigation of title, &c. Moreover, the difficulties and expense of transfer are usually very great : as each purchaser has to undergo the same labor and expense. If the debtor fails to pay, the process of obtaining redress or possession of the land is usually very troublesome and expensive. The consequence of all these obstacles is, of course, to raise greatly the terms on which money can be borrowed on mortgage

The system of Government Funds suggested to Büring the idea of creating a similar species of Land Stock. The Government could usually borrow much cheaper than the landlords, because the title was sure and indisputable, and there was no impediment to the negotiability of their Debts

Büring, therefore, conceived the idea of substituting the joint guarantee of all the proprietors for that of individuals : and establishing a book in which the Land Stock should be registered and be made transferable : and the dividends paid exactly in the same way as in the Public Funds. The Credit of the Association was, therefore, always interposed between the lenders and the borrowers. Those who bought the Stock looked only to the Association for the payment of their dividends: and the borrowers paid all interest to the Association, which took upon itself all questions of title and security. The whole of these Obligations are turned into Stock, transferable in all respects like the Public Funds. Such is the general design of these Associations : they avoid the rock of creating Paper Money : while they greatly facilitate the application of Capital to the land. They, in fact, do nothing more than turn Mortgages into Stock

These Associations are of two classes. The first are private Associations : and these again are divided into Companies formed by borrowers : and those formed by lenders. The second are founded by the State, or the provincial authorities

The system was introduced into Silesia in 1770 : Brandenburg in 1777 : Pomerania in 1781 : Hamburg in 1782 : West Prussia in 1787 : East Prussia in 1788 : Luneberg in 1791 : Esthonia and Livonia in 1803 : Schleswick-Holstein in 1811 : Mecklenberg in 1818 : Posen in 1822 : Poland in 1825 : Kalenburg, Grubenhagen, and Hildesheim in 1826 : Wurtemberg in 1827 : Hesse Cassel in 1832 : Westphalia in 1835 : Gallicia in 1841 : Hanover in 1842 : Saxony in 1844 : and France in 1852

The fullest information respecting these banks is to be found in a work by M. Josseau, from which these details are taken, and to which we may refer the reader who wants fuller information on the different constitutions of these Associations

All these Land Banks make advances to about one-half the value of the land, in small bonds chiefly varying from £5 to £100, bearing interest from $3\frac{1}{2}$ to 4 per cent., transferable by indorsement or delivery : together with a small sum to form a sinking fund to redeem the principal and defray the expenses of management

The holder of the bonds has as security for their payment the whole Capital of the company, and the lands specially mortgaged to them

The borrowers may pay either in money or in the bonds of the company which they may purchase from the public : thus exhibiting another example of the universal doctrine that the Release of a Debt is equivalent to a Payment in Money

These institutions have had the most marvelous effects in developing the agriculture of the countries in which they have been formed : exactly similar to the effects of Cash Credits in Scotland

Their Obligations have maintained through all crises—monetary, war, and revolutionary—a steadiness of value far beyond any other public securities whatever, either Government or Commercial. Josseau says that in a population of 27,827,990, the negotiable *Lettres de Gage,* or *Pfandbriefe,* amounted to 540,423,158 francs. In the revolutionary period of 1848, while the Prussian Funds fell to 69 : the shares of the Bank of Prussia to 63 : and the shares in railroads from 30 to 90 per cent. : the Land Bank Bonds producing 3½ per cent. interest stood at 93 in Silesia and Pomerania : at 83 in West Prussia : and at 96 in East Prussia

How Mercantile Bills of Exchange are **Paid**

24. We have now to show how erroneous are the ideas of those writers who, like Torrens and Mill, think that all Bills of Exchange are paid in Money and Bank Notes

All merchants and traders not only buy goods on Credit : but they also sell them on Credit. Hence, they are not only indebted on their own acceptances to those from whom they have bought the goods : but they hold the acceptances of those to whom they have sold goods

Now when a merchant knows that his own acceptances are coming due, and that he has not sufficient on his own account to meet them, he has only two methods of providing for them. He must either sell his goods in the market, or he must discount the acceptances he holds with his banker. The latter, is of course the preferable plan. Accordingly when his balance is low, and his own acceptances are falling due, he simply takes a batch of the acceptances he holds, and discounts them with his banker, who creates a Credit, a Debt, a Right of action, or a **Deposit** in his favor : and thus increases his balance

The merchant of course makes his own acceptances payable at his bankers' : consequently on the day on which they mature and become **Debts,** they are simply Cheques. And the whole mass of Cheques and Bills pass through the Clearing House, and as we

F 2

have shown in the description of the operations there, the whole transactions are settled : and settled by pure Transfers of Credit, without the use of a single Coin or Bank Note

Hence, in our present highly organised system of Credit, Bills of Exchange are not paid in Money or Bank Notes at all—except only in a very few isolated cases—but they are paid exclusively by the constant creation of new **Banking Credits**

Hence, in our present system, the constant creation of Banking Credits is a matter of vital necessity. If the London Bankers were suddenly to give notice that next day they would stop discounting, the result would be that 19 out of 20 merchants would stop payment

But more than that. As the merchants would, of course, exhaust all their means to maintain themselves, they would instantly draw their balances : and thus the bankers would draw upon themselves a **Run for Gold**

It is perfectly well understood by all bankers that *an* **Excessive Restriction** *of* **Credit** *causes and produces a* **Run** *for* **Gold**. And thus bankers and merchants will all come down together in one universal crash

The truth of this is now perfectly well known: and will be shown in a future chapter to be verified by numerous instances : and will have to be fully discussed in explaining the policy and effects of the Bank Charter Act of 1844

As, therefore, the constant and uninterrupted creation of Banking Credits is an indispensable necessity to maintain the existence both of merchants and bankers, we shall have to consider under what conditions they are to be created

On the Right of Foreign Banks to open Branches in London

25. We think it expedient to consider here a question which made a considerable stir some years ago—namely, the Right of Foreign Banks to open branches in London

In 1865, the National Bank of Scotland opened a branch in London, and the Bank of Scotland in 1872. The Charter of the Royal Bank did not permit it to bank out of Scotland : but in 1873, it obtained a Private Act, 36 and 37 Vict., c. ccxvii., with the full consent of the Bank of England and the English bankers, to enable it to open a branch in London, and carry on banking business there, except only issuing Notes. The bill was carried through Parliament by Mr. Goschen : and the branch was opened in August, 1874. These were the only Scotch Banks which had then opened branches in London : and up to that time they had evoked no open hostility from the English bankers

But in 1873, in consequence of the increasing connection between Glasgow and Cumberland, the Clydesdale Bank opened three branches in Cumberland at Carlisle, Whitehaven, and Workington. This invasion of the English provinces by a Scotch Bank, excited the vehement opposition of the English bankers, both private and Joint Stock, and in April, 1874, Mr. Goschen who had carried the bill of the Royal Bank through Parliament in 1873, at their instance brought in a bill to extrude the Scotch Banks from England

Now, in these days of free competition : and as, for the purposes of trade and commerce, England and Scotland are one country, it seems somewhat surprising that this right should be questioned. No one questions the rights of English Banks to open branches in Scotland, if they choose to do so : and, in fact, several of the English Colonial banks have agencies in Scotland. Why, then, should it be supposed that it is contrary to law for the Scotch Banks to open branches in any part of England ?

Many of the Scotch Insurance Offices have opened branches in London, and other parts of England, and not a word of objection was ever offered by the English Insurance Offices. Why, then, should the right of the Scotch Banks to open branches in England be questioned, and their doing so excite ill feeling on the part of English bankers ?

The gravamen of the case lies in this. When the monopoly of the Bank of England was first broken up in 1826, it was provided that Joint-Stock Banks might be founded in the provinces, and issue Notes : but not within 65 miles of London.

If they carried on Banking business in London they were obliged to discontinue their issue of Notes in the provinces

Now, the National Provincial Bank was a great provincial Bank, and issued large amounts of Notes in the provinces. But it deemed it expedient to commence banking in London : and, by the terms of the Act of 1826, it was obliged to give up its provincial issues of Notes. The union of Banks now called the Capital and Counties Bank also became London bankers, and they were also obliged to give up their provincial issues. And these banks and their fellow English bankers thought it extremely hard that they should have to give up their issues of notes when commencing banking in London, while the Scotch Banks could maintain their issues in Scotland, when they equally did London business

It was somewhat strange, however, that, while so much ill feeling was aroused against the Scotch Banks, not a word was ever said against the National Bank of Ireland, which not only has its head office and eight branches in London, and still maintains an authorised circulation of notes in Ireland greater than all the Scotch Banks put together

Mr. Stephen Cave, on behalf of the Goverment, moved an amendment to the second reading of Mr. Goschen's bill, that a select Committee should be appointed to consider and report upon the restrictions imposed, and privileges conferred by law on bankers authorised to make and issue notes in England, Scotland and Ireland respectively, which was carried without a division

This Committee began its sittings on the 19th April, 1875, and took evidence during 21 days; and reported the evidence to the House : but made no report on the evidence taken and recommended its re-appointment in the next session. But this was not done. And the result was, as is invariably the case with Parliamentary Committees and Royal Commissions on such subjects, they left the matter exactly as it was

The primary object of the Committee was to ascertain the legality, or the contrary, of the Scotch bankers opening branches in London. It examined personally two very eminent Counsel,

Mr. Fitzjames Stephen, Q.C., now Mr. Justice Stephen, and Sir Henry Thring, C.B., Parliamentary draughtsman to the Government, now Lord Thring, as to the state of the law : and besides that they had the written opinions of Sir James Scarlett (Lord Abinger), Sir Edward Sugden (Lord St. Leonards), Mr. Richards, and Mr. Roundell Palmer (Lord Selborne)

We shall commence by stating the opinions given by these Counsel

Mr. Stephen gave it as his opinion among other points that " No joint-stock bank which issues notes anywhere, except the joint stock banks in England and more than 65 miles from London, may carry on business in any part of England "

He considered that all "foreign banks whatever including under the name 'foreign' not only Continental Banks but British Banks out of England : that is, Scotch, Irish, and Colonial Banks are forbidden by the Acts of Parliament to establish themselves in any part of England." (Q. 206)

He denied, for example, that the Bank of Amsterdam could open a branch in London.   (Q. 207)

Mr. Stephen admitted that he had never turned his attention to the question before : and that he had merely been instructed to look at the matter on behalf of the English bankers some two days or a week previously : and that he was somewhat biased by the side on which he was called.   He also said that he had derived most of his information from the memorandum of Sir Henry Thring, to be mentioned immediately

Sir Henry Thring differed so far from Mr. Stephen that he thought the Scotch Banks might open branches in the provinces beyond the 65 miles limit, though he spoke somewhat doubtfully (Q. 404, 406).   But he agreed with Mr. Stephen that it was illegal to open branches in London or within the limit of 65 miles

He also presented a memorandum to the committee containing numerous references to the second edition of my *Theory and Practice of Banking*, and stating certain general conclusions he had arrived at—" Such being the circumstances of the case, the first question is whether it is or it is not legal for Scotch Joint-

Stock Company Banks of issue to establish branches in England ? In answer to that question, it is submitted that the prohibitions contained in the Acts of 1697 and 1708, and repeated in 1800, are still in force, with the special modification introduced by the Act of 1826, and are perfectly general in their terms, and extend to Scotch Banks of issue, as well as to country banks of issue in England : and consequently that with the exception of the Royal Bank of Scotland, which is empowered by Act of Parliament to have a branch in London, all other branches belonging to Scotch banks of issue in London, or within 65 miles thereof, are illegal. On the other hand, there does not appear to be any legal prohibition against the Clydesdale Banking Company establishing their branches in Cumberland, being at a distance of more than 65 miles from London "

Sir Henry Thring then presented some suggestions as to the policy of expelling the Clydesdale Bank by law from Cumberland, which we need not discuss, as of course every one is entitled to have his own opinion as to expediency and policy : and happily any such attempt would now be utterly abortive

Having been expressly selected by the Royal Commissioners for the Digest of the Law to declare the law on all points relating to Bank Notes, and, moreover, having been frequently referred to in Sir Henry Thring's memorandum : and though I should have had the highest respect for the opinions of the learned counsel examined in matters with which they were more familiar—but being satisfied that in this instance their opinions were erroneous, I applied to the Chancellor of the Exchequer to be heard before the Committee : but he did not accede to my request. However, as the opinions given by the learned counsel struck at such wide-spread interests, I addressed a letter to the *Daily News*, which appeared on the 8th May, 1875, showing that it was perfectly legal for the Scotch Banks to open branches in any part of England, so long as they did not issue notes in England

There were also published in the appendix the opinions given in 1833 by Sir James Scarlett, Sir Edward Sugden, and Mr. Griffiths, on the question whether Joint-Stock Banks of Deposit could be established in London previously to the clause in the Bank Charter Act of 1833. These three counsel held that they could not : they maintained that the words of the monopoly clause of 1697 and subsequent Acts included Banks of Deposit as well as of issue. But Sir John Campbell, the Attorney-General, held the reverse : he held that the monopoly of the Bank of England was strictly confined to issuing notes : and that it was perfectly legal at Common Law to establish Joint-Stock Banks of Deposit. And upon that opinion the Government acted, and introduced the declaratory clause in the Bank Charter Act of 1833

In 1855 the Clydesdale Bank took the opinion of Mr. Roundell Palmer (Lord Selborne) as to whether it was legal for them to open branches in London and other parts of England, and to carry on banking business, except only as to issuing notes. Mr. Palmer gave it as his opinion that it was perfectly legal for them to do so. The opinion of Lord Selborne, therefore, exactly agreed with the opinion I published in the *Daily News* of the 8th May, 1875

The case is an example of the futility of Committees of the House of Commons undertaking to investigate and determine questions of pure Law, on which the most eminent Counsel are in diametrical contradiction to each other

We have now to put the question on its purely legal basis. It entirely turns on the privileges of the Bank of England : and it necessary to state exactly what these privileges are

The privileges of the Bank of England are a penal enactment against the rights of the rest of the trading community : and, therefore, they are to be construed in the strictest manner possible. Nothing is contrary to Law except what is clearly and distinctly forbidden by it : everything else is legal and permissible

At its first institution the Bank of England received no monopoly. The Act of 1697 only provided that no other Bank should be established by Parliament. In 1709 it was enacted that no company or society exceeding six persons might borrow, owe, or take up any sum or sums of money on their bills or notes payable at demand, or at any time less than six months from the borrowing thereof, in that part of Great Britain called England

At that time no one had framed a definition of Banking. But it was supposed that issuing notes payable on demand was what so essentially constituted Banking, that to prevent them from doing that was to prevent them from banking

In 1742, to strengthen this monopoly more effectually it was enacted that—" To prevent any doubts that may arise concerning the privilege or power given by former Acts of Parliament to the said Governor and Company of **Exclusive Banking,** and also in regard to the erecting any other Bank, or Banks, by Parliament, or restraining other persons from **Banking** during the continuance of the said privilege granted to the Governor and Company of the Bank of England, as before recited, it is hereby further enacted and declared, by the authority aforesaid, that it is the true intent and meaning of the Act that no other Bank shall be erected, established, or allowed by Parliament, and that it shall not be lawful for any body politic or corporate whatsoever, united, or to be united, in covenants or partnership exceeding the number of six persons, in that part of Great Britain called **England,** to borrow, owe, or take up any sum or sums of money on their Bills or Notes payable at demand, or at any less time than six months from the borrowing thereof, during the continuance of such said privilege of the said Governor and Company, who are hereby declared to be and to remain a Corporation, with the privilege of Exclusive Banking as aforesaid "

These words, which were always contained in subsequent Bank Charter Acts, strictly define the privilege of the Bank of England. Its sole monopoly is that no Bank having more than six (now ten) partners shall issue notes in England payable at less than six months : but all other kinds of Banks and banking are left absolutely free

There is no doubt whatever that Parliament intended to confer an absolute monopoly of banking on the Bank of England : but by strictly defining what they conceived banking to consist in, they ultimately defeated their own purpose. There was no instance at that time of any bank which did not issue its own notes, nor any idea that a Bank could be carried on without issuing notes. If there had been, Parliament would certainly have provided against it. If the words had been general, and had given a simple monopoly of banking, no other bank of any sort or description exceeding six persons could have carried on business in England. They did not, and could not be expected to foresee that banking could be carried on without issuing notes. In order to make assurance doubly sure they gave what they conceived to be a description of banking : and the legal effect of so doing is to restrict the monopoly alone to that particular method of banking so described

After the crisis of 1825 the Bank consented to give up a portion of their monopoly : and in 1826 Joint-Stock Banks were allowed to be formed, and issue notes beyond the limit of 65 miles from London : provided that they had no office and did no business in London. If they did business in London they were obliged to give up their provincial issues

About 1793 the London bankers of their own accord discontinued issuing notes : and showed, what had never been imagined before, that in some places banking, or at least some kinds of it, can be carried on without issuing notes. About 1820 some Economists began to scrutinise the Bank Charter Acts, and maintained that Joint-Stock Banks might be established, and carry on their business in the then manner of London bankers, without issuing notes, which would be no infringement of the privileges of the Bank. A declaratory clause to that effect was inserted in the Bank Charter Act of 1832 : and in consequence of this discovery, and this declared common law right, the London Joint-Stock Banks were founded

Such is a simple statement of the law of the case. And with respect to the Scotch Banks opening branches in London or any other part of England, the sole question is—Do they issue notes payable at less than six months in England ? The clear answer is that they do not : and consequently they have an undoubted right to open branches in London or any other part of England if they choose. It would be perfectly legal for them to remove their head offices to London, and maintain their issues in Scotland, as the National Bank of Ireland has its head office and several branches in London, and maintains its issues in Ireland. And as a matter of fact any bank in any part of the world has a legal right to open branches in London, or in any part of England, so long as it does not issue notes payable in less than six months after issue in England

No doubt it is a great grievance that the National Provincial Bank was obliged to abandon its lucrative country issues on commencing business in London : as the Capital and Counties Bank has also had to do : and as every provincial bank will have to do that establishes its head office in London. But whatever the hardship and the injustice of the case may be, the remedy does not lie in depriving the Scotch Banks of their legal rights, but rather in the revision and rectification of the chaotic mass of absurdity of the present banking system of England which the logic of events will assuredly force on the Government

On the Economical Effects of Banking

26. Having now given an exposition of the actual mechanism of the different kinds of Banks, and shown the entire erroneousness of the notions of Banking which are still prevalent in this country, we can observe its Economical effects

The business of a Bank is not to borrow Money from one set of persons to lend to another—it is to build up a superstructure of Credit on a given basis of Bullion several times exceeding its amount : which Credit is intended to circulate and produce all the effects of money

And every one who has understood the mechanism of Banking has seen that it practically augments the Capital of the Country

Thus John Law says that the Bank of Scotland on a basis of £10,000 in money was able to maintain £50,000 of its notes in circulation : which he says was equivalent to so much additional money to the country

He also says—"The introduction of Credit by means of a Bank augments the quantity of Money more in one year than a prosperous commerce would do in ten"

So Bishop Berkeley, after proposing many wise queries on Money and Credit, says that a Bank is a Gold Mine, and asks whether it be not the true philosopher's stone ?

Alexander Hamilton, the celebrated financier of the United States, in presenting a Report to Congress on the advantages of founding a National Bank says—

" The following are among the principal advantages of a Bank—

"First : the augmentation of the active or Productive Capital of a country . . . . It is a well established fact that Banks in good Credit can circulate a far greater sum than the actual quantum of their Capital in gold and silver . . . . . This faculty is produced in various ways—

"(1) A great portion of the Notes which are issued and pass current as cash are indefinitely suspended in circulation from the confidence which each holder has that he can, at any moment, turn them into gold and silver

" (2) Every loan which a Bank makes is, in its first shape, a Credit given to the borrower in its books, the amount of which it stands ready to pay, either in its own notes, or gold or silver, at his option. But in a great number of cases no actual payment is made in either . . . . . The same circumstances illustrate the truth of the position that it is one of the properties of banks to *increase the active Capital of a country*. This additional employment given to money, and the faculty of a bank to lend and circulate a greater sum than the amount of coin, are to all the purposes of trade and industry an absolute **Increase** of **Capital**. Purchases and undertakings in general can be carried on by means of Bank Paper or Credit as effectually as by an equal sum of gold and silver. And thus, by contributing to enlarge the mass of industrious and commercial enterprises, banks become nurseries of national wealth—a consequence as satisfactorily verified by experience as it is clearly deducible in theory "

So J. B. Say says—" If Bills of Credit could replace completely metallic money it is evident that a Bank of Circulation veritably augments the sum of National Wealth, because in this case, the metallic wealth, becoming superfluous as an agent of circulation, and nevertheless preserving its own value, becomes disposable, and can serve other purposes.   But how does that substitution take place ? What are its limits ? What classes of society make their profit of this interest of the new fund added to the Capital of the nation ?

"According as a bank issues its Notes, and the public consents to receive them on the same footing as metallic money, the number of monetary units increases

" If, suppose, it issues one hundred millions of Notes, it will withdraw, perhaps, forty millions in specie, which it will put in reserve to meet the payments which may be demanded of it. Therefore, if it adds to the quantity of money in circulation, and if it withdraws forty millions from circulation, it is as if it added only sixty millions

" We now wish to learn what class of society enjoys the use of this **New Capital**"

Say then goes on to explain how this **New Capital** is employed, and who reaps the benefit of it

And J. B. Say is the writer who said that those say that Credit is Capital maintain that the same thing can be in two places at once !!

Gilbart says—" Bankers also employ their own **Credit** as **Capital**. They issue Notes promising to pay the bearer on demand.   As long as the public are willing to take these Notes as gold, they produce the same effects.   The banker who makes advances to the agriculturist, the manufacturer, or the merchant, in his own Notes, stimulates as much the productive powers of the country, and provides employment for as many laborers as if by means of the philosopher's stone, he had created an equal amount of solid gold.   It is this feature of our banking system that has been most frequently assailed.   It has been called a system of fictitious Credit—a raising the wind—a system of bubbles.   Call it what you please, we will not quarrel with names : but by what-ever name you please to call it, it is a powerful instrument of production.   If it be a fictitious system, its effects are not fictitious : for it leads to the feeding, the clothing, and the employing of a numerous population.   If it be a raising of the wind : it is the wind of commerce, that bears to distant markets the produce of our soil, and wafts to our shores, the productions of every climate. If it be a system of bubbles, they are bubbles which, like those of steam move the mighty engines that promote a nation's greatness, and a nation's wealth"

What Gilbart says about notes is all true: but he omits to mention that Banking Credits circulated by means of Cheques, have exactly the same effects as Banking Credits which are circulated by means of Notes

We shall have something more to say as to the effects of Banking in the next chapter

Demolition of the " Wages Fund *" Theory*

27. The exposition we have given of the actual mechanism of Banking demolishes a theory which was long held by Economists, and commonly called the " Wages Fund Theory " : though we believe that all Economists of repute have now abandoned it

A considerable number of Economists stoutly maintained that Wealth was to be restricted to material things only, such as Money

They then contended that Wages are paid exclusively in material Money, and they called the quantity of Money paid in Wages the " Wages Fund," and maintained that it could not be exceeded. Capital they insisted was composed only of material things, the savings of the past

They then maintained that Wages depend on the ratio between population and Capital

Now this was an error to begin with: because all the Money spent as Wages is not used as Capital, *i.e.*, expended with the intention of making a profit by it

A very large portion of Money spent as Wages is not Capital but an expenditure of Income. Thus the wages of domestic servants, and the money paid for professional services of all sorts is not Capital but the expenditure of Income

Wages only spent for the purpose of profit: such as agricultural, manufacturing, and commercial Wages: are Capital

Now there is an important difference between Wages spent as Income, and Wages laid out as Capital. In the former case there is no limit to them but the absolute rule of Supply and Demand: in the latter there is

If I want professional services of the highest order there is no limit to the price which must be paid. A surgical operation of great delicacy, which may only last a minute, may perhaps cost £150, when performed by a person of the most eminent skill. On one occasion a very eminent counsel received £2,000 for half-an-hour's work. So the wages paid to servants of all sorts are only determined by the Law of Supply and Demand

But when Wages are laid out as Capital the case is different. In such cases the amount which a Capitalist can afford to pay as wages is limited and controlled by the profits which he expects to make by the sale of the product. If the price of the product could be forced up indefinitely, wages might no doubt be forced up indefinitely. But that is very far from being the case. No expenditure upon a product can force up its price indefinitely. The value of the product is solely governed by the great general Law of Supply and Demand. And as no Capitalist can continue to produce for any length of time unless he receives usual profits : he cannot afford to give more as Wages than will allow him to obtain that profit. Hence, if he cannot reduce wages he must cease to produce. Thus, in all cases of Wages expended as Capital, there is a natural cast-iron limit which they cannot exceed, however much they may fall short of it.

We shall now allow the originators of the Wages Fund Theory to speak for themselves

Senior says that the proximate cause which decides the rate of Wages is the extent of the **Fund** [What Fund ?] for the maintenance of laborers compared with the numbers of laborers to be maintained

Jones, who expressly confines Wealth to material objects only, says that Wages depend on the amount of Wealth devoted to maintaining laborers

" The amount of Wealth devoted to the maintenance of Labor constitutes the Labor Fund of the world, and the amount so devoted in any country constitutes the Labor Fund of that country

" The third division of the Labor fund consists of what is properly called Capital, that is of the stored-up results of past Labor, used with a view to profit "[1]

Mill says[2]—" Since, therefore, the rate of Wages which results from competition, distributes the whole Wages Fund among the whole laboring population "

So, Mill lays it down as a fundamental proposition that " Industry is limited by Capital." But what intelligible meaning can be given to this expression unless we first distinctly define what Capital is?

All the writers who support the Wages Fund Theory affirm that it consists of Capital, which they say is only the accumulation of the savings of the *past*. They maintain that it is only increased Capital that can lead to the increased employment of labor, and that that increased Capital can only arise from the increased savings of the past

But is this the fact? Are Wages only paid out of Money which is the result of past savings? Are Wages paid only in specie? No one who has the slightest acquaintance with practical business can fail to perceive that such an idea is altogether erroneous. Every practical man knows that enormous masses of Wages are paid in Credit

Mill himself says[3]—" When Paper Currency [*i.e.*, Credit] is supplied in our country by bankers and banking companies, the amount is almost wholly turned into **Productive Capital** . . . So employed, it yields, like any other **Capital**, wages of labor, and profits of stock . . . The **Capital** itself, in the long run, becomes entirely wages, and when replaced by the sale of the produce, becomes Wages again: thus affording a perpetual fund for the maintenance of Productive labor: and increasing the annual produce of the Country by all that can be produced by the means of a **Capital** of that value "

[1] *Lectures on Political Economy*, pp. 114, 414, 415, 420
[2] *Princ. of Pol. Econ.*, Bk. ii., c. 12
[3] *Principles of Pol. Econ.*, Bk. ii., c. 12, § 5

G

He also says[1]—"An effect of this latter character naturally attends some extensions of **Credit**, especially when taking the form of **Bank Notes** or other instruments of Exchange. The additional **Bank Notes** are, in ordinary course, first issued to producers and dealers, to be employed as **Capital**"

These are the doctrines which we have shown fully exemplified in the operations of the Cash Credits of the Scotch Banks. The whole of the agricultural improvements, Canals, Docks, Harbours, Railways, and Public Buildings were constructed by laborers: and whence was the Fund provided which furnished their Wages? Simply from the Banks issuing their £1 Notes

And yet it is the very same Mill who sneers at the imbecility and the confused ideas of those who say that Credit may be used as Capital!

"Credit," he says,[2] "has a great, but not, as many people seem to suppose, a magical power: it cannot make something out of nothing. *How often is an extension of Credit talked of as equivalent to a creation of Capital, or as if Credit were actually Capital!!*"

Mill also asserts that Credit is not Productive power, in flat contradiction to his admissions in the preceding paragraphs

Thus, we see at every turn in Economics, the indispensable necessity of establishing clear and distinct concepts and definitions of Wealth, Credit, Capital, &c. Modern Commerce is utterly unintelligible unless **Credit** is included under the term **Capital**: and the doctrine that Industry is limited by Capital is entirely false, if Capital be restricted only to Money, the realised savings of the past

The Wages Fund consists of **Money**, together with **Credit**—the realised profits of the past, together with the expected profits of the future: as we have over and over again set forth—*Every future profit has a* **Present Value**—and that **Present Value** may be brought into Commerce and made Capital of as part of the Wages Fund; exactly in the same way as Money, the accumulation of the past

[1] *Principles of Pol. Econ.*, Bk. iii., c. 2, § 1, Note
[2] *Ibid.*, Bk. iii., c. 11, § 1

On John Stuart Mill's notions on Banking and Currency

28. Having now given an exposition of the actual mechanism and Economical effects of Banking, we are constrained to contrast them with the dogmas of John Stuart Mill, not from any love of controversy, which we cordially dislike, but simply because Mill's work is the one which is still usually put into the hands of unfortunate students of Economics

Mill says[1]—"Further consideration showed that the uses of Money are in no respect promoted by increasing the quantity which exists and circulates in a country : the service which it performs being as well rendered by a small as by a large aggregate amount "

This certainly is somewhat startling doctrine. If only a certain quantity of work could be done such a dogma might have some degree of plausibility. But is it not possible to develope new works and new industry by means of introducing new Capital ? According to this dogma the introduction of new Capital into a country can do it no service. But is such a dogma consistent with the facts ? It is usually supposed that the very thing which poor countries like Ireland, Scotland, and India want is the introduction of fresh Capital. Of course if the introduction of fresh Capital can do no good, the withdrawal of Capital can do no harm

Has not the prodigious increase of the Wealth of Scotland during the last 150 years been due entirely to the Cash Credits of the Scotch Banks ? And the same is true also of Ireland. Have not most of the Indian railways been constructed mainly by the supplies of British Capital poured into the country ? If the Scotch system of Banking could be gradually and cautiously introduced into India, it would give a prodigious stimulus to the Wealth of India : and perhaps even render her independent of British Capital

Mill again says[2]—"Another of the fallacies from which the advocates of an inconvertible currency derive support is the notion that an increase of the currency quickens industry. This idea was set afloat by Hume in his essay on Money, and has had many devoted adherents since "

[1]*Prelim. Rem.*, p. 4   [2]Bk. iii., ch. xiii., § 6

G 2

Any one who had the least experience of practical business, and will study the practical effects of Banking, knows that it is no fallacy at all that an increase of Capital, either by the introduction of fresh Money, or by the creation of Credit within legitimate limits, quickens industry. But, of course, this does not mean Credit without limit : but Credit created within certain strictly defined scientific limits

Mill's dogmas would certainly not meet with acceptance from statesmen or from practical men of business

Mill further says[1]—"A banker's profession being that of a **Money Lender,** his issue of Notes is a simple *extension* of his ordinary occupation "

We have shown that it is a total misconception of the nature of the business of banking to say that it consists in **Lending Money.** The business of a banker consists in buying Money and Debts, by creating other Debts, which may exceed several times the amount of Cash he holds, which may be circulated either by means of Bank Notes or Cheques : and are equivalent in all respects to the creation of an equal amount of Money

Issuing Bank Notes, therefore, is not an *extension* of a banker's ordinary business. It is the very essence of his business. Formerly, banking was defined to consist in issuing Notes. But, in the present day, Cheques have to an immense extent superseded Bank Notes. The very essence of Banking is to create Credit : and whether these Credits are circulated by means of Notes, or Cheques, in no way alters the nature of Banking, but is a pure matter of convenience

Mill then says[2]—"But if the Paper Currency is convertible, coin may still be obtained from the issuers in exchange for Notes. All additional Notes, therefore, which are attempted to be forced into circulation after the metals have been completely superseded, will return upon the issuers in exchange for coin "

He also says[3]—"When metallic money had been entirely superseded and expelled from circulation by the substitution of an equal amount of Bank Notes, any attempt to keep a still

[1]Bk. iii., ch. 22, § 2   [2]Bk. iii., ch. 13, § 1   [3]Bk. iii., ch. 22, § 3

further quantity of Paper in circulation must, if the Notes be convertible, be a complete failure. The metals would, as before, be required for exportation, and would, for that purpose, be demanded from the Banks to the full extent of the superfluous Notes, which thus could not possibly remain in circulation "

The preposterous folly of these dogmas is shown by the fact that when the Bank of Scotland was founded, although it was the only Bank in Scotland, upon a deposit of £10,000 in money by shareholders, it was able to maintain £50,000 of its Notes in circulation

At the present day the English Joint Stock Banks usually keep a reserve of about one tenth in cash to support the circulation of their Credits

But in Scotland where the system of Credit is more perfectly and highly organised than in England, the Banks only find it necessary to keep cash to the one twenty-second part of their Credits in various forms

According to Mill's dogmas such a state of things would be impossible : but all the Credit created in excess of the Cash held would at once return upon the Banks for payment

Mill then says[1]—" The substitution of Paper for Metallic Currency is a national gain: any further increase of Paper beyond this is *a form of* **Robbery** !

" An issue of Notes is a manifest gain to the issuers, who, until the Notes are returned for payment, obtain the use of them as if they were real Capital, and so long as the Notes are no permanent addition to the Currency, but merely supersede gold or silver to the same amount, the gain of the issuers is a loss to no one : it is obtained by saving to the community the expense of the more costly material. But if there be no gold or silver to be superseded—if the Notes are **added** to the Currency, instead of being substituted for the metallic portion of it—all holders of Currency lose by the depreciation of its value the exact equivalent of what the issuers gain "

Now Mill asserts that for a Banker to create Credit in excess of the Cash he holds is Robbery

[1]Bk. iii., ch. 13, Sec. 5

But all profits in Banking are made by creating Credit in excess of Cash

Therefore all profits made in Banking are Robbery ! !

Certainly, Mill is an Economist who ought to be very popular among bankers

But if it is robbery for bankers to create Credit in excess of the gold they hold, it must be equally robbery for merchants to create Credit in excess of the gold they hold

Now merchants create Credit, not because they have gold at the time they create it : but because they expect to be in possession of gold, or its equivalent, at the time the bill falls due

We have shown that Say, Hamilton, Gilbart, and all persons practically conversant with the mechanism of banking, declare that if a Bank can maintain in circulation a quantity of Credit in excess of the Cash it holds, that is, for all practical purposes, an augmentation of the Capital of the country

But, Mill declares that it is **Robbery**

Such is the beautiful harmony of doctrine among Economists

We have now pursued our distasteful task sufficiently far to show what an untrustworthy guide Mill is on all matters relating to Banking and the Currency.   If we had chosen, we could have shown his inconsistencies and self-contradictions at much greater length : but that would have been far too great a tax upon the patience of our readers : and what we have shown is amply sufficient for our purpose

CHAPTER VIII

ON THE FOREIGN EXCHANGES

Definition of an **Exchange**

1. An " **Exchange** " in commerce is, when a person pays a Debt he owes to his Creditor by transferring to him a Debt due to him from some one else

It is a *Delegatio :* or one form of *Novatio*

Thus, where a person pays his Creditor by a Cheque on his banker, or by a Bank Note, or a Bill of Exchange on another person, it is an " **Exchange** "

Two passengers are travelling in an omnibus. The fare is sixpence. One passenger pays the conductor a shilling. The conductor is then indebted to that passenger in sixpence. The other passenger has a sixpence in his hand ready to pay his fare. The conductor, by a nod, tells him to give the sixpence to the first passenger. By this operation both Debts are paid. The Debt of the conductor to the first passenger : and the Debt of the second passenger to the conductor : are paid by one operation. The whole transaction is an " **Exchange** "

Three parties and two Debts are thus necessary to an " Exchange "

The " Exchanges " is that branch of commerce which treats of the remission and settlement of Debts between parties living in different places either within or beyond the limits of the same country : and of the Exchange of the Money of one country for that of another

The state of the Exchanges between any two places or countries depends upon two distinct things—

1. The state of the Moneys of the two places

2. The state of the Commercial dealings between the two places

The state of the Exchanges, which depends upon the state of the Moneys of the two places, is called the **Nominal Exchange**

The state of the Exchanges, which depends on the Commercial dealings between the two places or countries, is termed the **Real** or the **Commercial Exchange**

On the Nominal Exchange

2. Suppose that the Coinages of two countries are made of the same Metal, and the Coinage of one country is taken as the standard : then the Quantity of the Coin of the other country, which contains exactly the same quantity of pure Metal, is called the Par of Exchange between the two countries

Suppose that the exchanges between England and France were estimated in gold. There is as near as possible one-fourth more pure Gold in an English sovereign than in a Napoleon, or French 20 franc piece

If the English sovereign were taken as the standard, it would be equal to 1·25 Napoleon : and 1·25 would be the Par of Exchange between England and France

The Exchanges between England and France are, however, estimated in francs, which are a silver coin. Moreover, the English sovereign is not exactly 1·25 Napoleon. Accordingly 25·21 was usually considered as the Par of Exchange between England and France, before the recent change in the relative value of Gold and Silver

On Bullion and Coin

3. We have in the first chapter explained the circumstances out of which the necessity for Money arose, and shown that Metal has advantages above every other substance to be made Money : and of Metals, Gold, Silver, and Copper have been chiefly preferred. Gold and Silver in a perfectly pure state, however, are too soft to be used for this purpose : and it is necessary to mix some other metal with them to harden them, which is called Alloy. By a chemical law, when two metals are mixed together, the mixture is harder than either of them in a pure state

Gold and silver in the mass are called **Bullion** : but as the laws of all countries which use Gold and Silver as Money define the quantity of Alloy which is to be mixed with the pure metal, we shall use the word Bullion to mean Gold and Silver in the mass, mixed with such a proportion of alloy as is ordered by law, so as to be fit to be made into Money

The purity of Gold is measured by 24th parts, termed Carats : and ever since the 6th Edward VI. (1553) the Bullion used for the gold coinage has been 22 carats of pure gold, and 2 carats of alloy. This is called Crown Gold

The standard of Silver Bullion was fixed by William the Conqueror at 11 ozs. 2 dwts. fine : or 222 dwts. of pure silver, and 18 dwts. of alloy. And, except during a short period of confusion, from the 34th Henry VIII. (1543) to Elizabeth, it has never been departed from. It is called the " Old right standard of England," or "Sterling" : and as the Sovereigns of England, though they reduced the weight of the coin, with the slight exception just mentioned, never tampered with the purity of the metal, Sterling came to signify honest and true, or to be depended upon

In France and those countries which have adopted a decimal coinage, Bullion is made of 9 parts of pure metal and 1 part alloy : but it is found in practice that the English proportion gives greater durability to the metal, and therefore is better adapted for a coinage

Some nations have used simple Bullion as money : but the merchants of those nations were obliged to carry about with them scales and weights to weigh out the Bullion on each occasion. This was usual among the Jews. In some countries it was necessary to weigh and assay the Bullion at each operation, which was of course a great impediment to commerce.

But about the eighth or ninth century B.C., Pheidon of Argos, the most powerful sovereign then in Greece, is said to have devised the plan of cutting the Bullion into pieces of a certain definite weight, and of affixing a stamp upon them to certify to the public that these pieces of Bullion were of a certain definite weight and fineness. These pieces of Bullion issued by public authority, with a stamp on them to certify their weight and fineness, and called by a definite name, and intended to be used in commerce without further examination, are called **Coins**

This stamp or certificate, of course, in no way affects the value of the metal, or the Quantity of things it will exchange for or purchase. Its only object is to save the trouble of weighing and assaying the Bullion in commercial transactions. Nor can the **Name** of the coin in any way affect its Value. Values, it is true, are estimated in the number of these pieces of Bullion or Coins : but it is necessarily implied in the bargain that the coins contain a certain quantity of Bullion of a certain fineness

It is also perfectly evident that if this process of stamping Bullion, and so turning it into coin, is done free of all expense : at the will of any one who chooses to present Bullion and demands to have it stamped : and also without any delay : the Value of the metal as Bullion must be exactly the same as the Value of the metal as coin

If, however, a charge is made for the workmanship : or if any tax is levied on changing the metal from one form into the other : or if any delay takes place in doing so : there will be a difference between the Value of the metal as Bullion and as Coin : equal to the charge for workmanship, the tax, and the amount of interest accruing during the period of delay

These, however, are all fixed or constant quantities, which may be ascertained : and they form the limits of the variation of the Value of the metal in one form from its Value in the other

In the following remarks we shall assume that there is no charge for the workmanship, no tax, and no delay in doing it : no obstruction, in short, of any sort, to changing the metal from one form to the other

Upon these assumptions then, and only on these, we have this fundamental Law of the Coinage—

Any Quantity of Metal in the form of **Bullion** *must be of exactly the same Value as the same Quantity of Metal in the form of* **Coin**

In the case of the Coinage of England, no charge of any sort is made for coining gold Bullion : but as considerable delay may happen before any one who brings Bullion to the Mint can have it coined, the 7 and 8 Vict. (1844) c. 32, s. 4, enacts that every person may take standard Bullion to the Bank of England, and that the Bank shall be obliged to give him Notes to the amount of £3 17s. 9d. for every ounce of such Bullion. And as the holder of such Notes may demand legal coin for them at the rate of £3 17s. 10½d. per ounce, there is thus practically a difference of 1½d. per ounce between Gold Bullion and Gold Coin

What is a Pound?

4. Sir Robert Peel once asked the question—" What is a Pound ? " and he found many who could give him no answer. We have now to explain how a certain weight of Gold Bullion has come to be called a **Pound**

The original Measure of Value in all the countries of Western Europe—France, England, Italy, Spain, Scotland—was the pound weight of Silver Bullion

No coin of this actual weight was ever struck : but the pound weight was divided into 240 coins, called Pence, or *Denarii :* twelve of these Pence were called a Shilling; or **Solidus** : and, therefore 20 Shillings, or *Solidi*, actually weighed a Pound of silver Bullion

Now, let us denote the Pound weight of metal in the form of Bullion by the symbol—℔ : and the Pound weight of metal in the form of Coin by the symbol—£ : then we have—

240 Pence = 20 Shillings = £1 = 1 ℔

Now, if the Pound weight of metal were divided into more than 240 pieces, it is clear that the greater number of pieces would still be equal to the Pound in weight : and, if we denoted 240 pieces by the symbol — £, irrespective of their weight, we should have the—℔ = £1 + the number of pieces above 240

This is what has been done in the Coinage of all the countries above-mentioned. The sovereigns of these various countries were frequently in want of money to pursue their various extravagances. As they could not increase the quantity of the metal, they adopted the fraudulent plan of surreptitiously cutting the Pound weight of Bullion into a greater number of pieces. But they still called them by the same name. By this means they gained an illusory augmentation of wealth. As they could not increase the quantity of the metal, they at various periods *falsified the certificate :* while they still called the coins by the same name. Thus the quantity of Bullion in each penny was diminished

The consequence of this was manifest. As 240 pence were called a Pound in money—or £—, whatever their weight was : and as more than 240 pence were coined out of the Pound weight of Bullion—or ℔—: the £, or Pound of metal in Coin, began to vary from the ℔, or Pound of metal in Bullion

Edward I. began this bad practice in 1300, and coined 243 pennies out of the Pound weight of metal : in 1344 Edward III. coined 266 pennies out of the Pound weight of metal : in 1412 Henry coined the Pound into 360 pennies : and so it gradually crept up, until Elizabeth, in 1601, coined the Pound weight into 744 pennies

Then we have manifestly—

744 pennies = 62 shillings = £3 2s. = 1 ℔

As there are 12 ounces in one Pound weight of Bullion, it is evident that each ounce was coined into 62 pence : and, as the value of Bullion is measured by the ounce, the Mint Price of Silver was said to be 5s. 2d. per ounce

In Scotland this Depreciation of the Coinage began about the same period as in England, but it proceeded to much greater lengths. In 1306 Robert Bruce coined the pound weight into

252 pennies : in 1451 James II. coined it into 760 pennies, or £3 4s.: and the depreciation was continued until at last, in 1738, the Pound weight was coined into 8,928 pennies, or £37 4s.: and, thus, the Pound Scots became equal to twenty pence

In France and Italy the Depreciation proceeded. twice as far as in Scotland. The French Livre and the Italian Lira were at last reduced to 10d. The French Livre, which is now called a franc, has been adopted as the basis of the decimal system of coinage : and the *solidus* has now dwindled down to the *sou*, or halfpenny

At the great recoinage in 1816, it was determined to adopt Gold as the standard coinage of England, and the Sovereign, or Pound in Gold, was coined to be equal to 20s. in Silver at the then market value of Gold and Silver

Ever since the time of Charles II. the coinage of Gold has been free to the public. But by the Act of 1816, the coinage of Silver and Bronze is retained in the hands of the Government. In order to obviate the effects of what is termed Gresham's Law, which will be described shortly, the value of Silver has been artificially raised. Since 1816 the Pound weight of Silver has been coined into 66 shillings : but four of these are retained for the expenses of coinage : and the 62 lighter shillings are declared to be of the same value as the previous heavier ones. Thus 20 of them are declared to be equal in value to the Sovereign or Pound : and thus their value is artificially raised about 6 per cent. But to prevent injustice being done they are not legal tender for any sum above 40s.: it having been intended to have made the Double Sovereign the monetary unit

The bronze coins are only worth about one-fourth part of their nominal value: pence and halfpence are only legal tender to the value of one shilling : and farthings to the value of sixpence

This country enjoys now the most admirable system of Coinage that was ever devised by the ingenuity of man : and as a proof of its excellence, while all the countries on the continent which attempted to make Gold and Silver equally legal tender to an unlimited amount when coined at a fixed ratio, were thrown into confusion and perturbation by the recent changes in the value of these metals, the coinage of this country passed through the whole of the protracted crisis with the most perfect tranquility.   He would be a bold and daring Minister indeed who would undertake to disturb our present system of Coinage

On the Meaning of the **Mint Price** of Gold and Silver

5. As the very purpose of coining is to certify that the pieces of Bullion are of a certain definite weight and fineness, it is evident that a fixed quantity of Bullion, such as a Pound Weight, must be divided into a fixed number of Coins

The **Number** *of* **Coins** *into which a given Quantity of Bullion is divided by Law is called the* **Mint Price** *of that Quantity of* **Bullion**

The Mint Price of Bullion is thus simply the amount of Coin which is equal to any quantity of Bullion, weight for weight

By the law at present in force, forty pounds weight of Standard Gold Bullion are divided into 1869 coins called Pounds or Sovereigns : hence one pound weight of Gold Bullion is coined into £46 14s. 6d. : or as the Value of Gold is measured by the ounce : one ounce of Gold Bullion is coined into £3 17s. 10½d.: and this is termed the **Mint Price** of Gold

The legal weight of the Pound, or Sovereign, is 5 dwts. $3\frac{171}{623}$ grs., or $113\frac{1}{623}$ grs. of pure gold. Sovereigns which fall below 5 dwts. $2\frac{3}{4}$ grs.: and half-sovereigns which fall below 2 dwts. $13\frac{1}{2}$ grs., cease to be legal tender

In the time of William the Conqueror the pound weight of Silver Bullion was coined into 240 pennies. Hence the Mint Price of silver was £1 per pound : but in the time of Elizabeth the pound weight of silver was coined in 744 pennies : hence, as 240 pennies is still called a £, the Mint Price of Silver then became £3 2s. per pound : or 5s. 2d. per ounce

To Alter *the* Mint Price *of Bullion is merely an expression which means an Alteration in the* Legal Weight *of the Coinage*

To suppose that the Mint Price of Bullion could vary is manifestly as great an error as to suppose that a hundredweight of sugar could be a different weight from 112 separate pounds weight of sugar : or that a quantity of wine in a hogshead could differ in quantity from the same quantity of wine in bottles : or that a loaf of bread could alter in its weight by being cut up into slices

It is not an Economic Error to Fix *the* Mint Price *of* Bullion

6. We must now say a word as to an error which is by no means infrequent. It is now acknowledged that it is a great Economic error to fix the Price of any articles. It used, formerly, to be the custom to fix wages and the price of various commodites by law: but all such attempts have long been abandoned as futile and mischievous. It is sometimes contended that it is an equal error to fix the **Mint Price** of **Gold**

But those who affirm this overlook a very important consideration. The word " Price," except in the single instance of " Mint Price," always denotes the quantity of the article which is used as a measure which is given for an article of a *different* nature. Thus, we say that the Price of a bushel of corn is 6s.: where the Silver, the substance in which prices are measured, is of a different nature from the corn

But, in the expression " Mint Price" of Bullion, it always means the Value of Bullion in Coin of the *same* metal. Thus the Mint Price of Gold Bullion means its weight in Gold Coin: the Mint Price of Silver Bullion means its weight in Silver Coin

Hence, by the very definition, the Mint Price of Gold and Silver Bullion merely means the identical quantity or weight of Gold or Silver Bullion in another form : and, by the very nature of things, the Mint Price of Bullion is a fixed quantity. If the

Law requires an ounce of gold to be coined into £3 17s. 10½d., that amount of coin must be of the same value as an ounce of gold, no matter whether gold becomes as plentiful as iron or as scarce as diamonds : for that quantity of Coin is always exactly equal to an ounce of Bullion : whatever be the abundance or scarcity of Bullion. The value of gold may vary with respect to other things : it may purchase more or less bread, or wine, or meat, at one time than another : but it is absolutely impossible that an ounce weight of gold in the form of Coin can differ from an ounce weight of gold in the form of Bullion. To suppose that it could, would be as irrational as to suppose that because bread became very abundant, or very scarce, a loaf of bread could differ from itself in weight when cut up into slices : or that a cask of wine could differ from itself when drawn off into bottles

The Mint Price of Gold, then, is nothing more than a public declaration of the weight of metal the Law requires to be in the Coin. An alteration of the Mint Price of Bullion means an alteration of the standard weight of the Coin : and would be the same thing in principle as an alteration in the standard yard measure. Those who ridicule the idea of having the Mint Price of Gold fixed, should, to be consistent, ridicule the idea of having the standard yard measure fixed

On the Meaning of the **Market Price** of Gold and Silver

7. The Mint Price of Bullion is, as we have seen, merely the number of Coins into which a certain quantity of Bullion is coined : consequently, so long as the coins contain their full legal weight of metal, they are always of the value of that quantity of Bullion

But when Coins have been some time in circulation they must necessarily lose some of their weight from the wear and tear of daily use, even if they be not subjected to any bad practices such as clipping, which used to be done to a great extent formerly in this country

But these coins may circulate for a considerable time in a country and lose a good deal of their weight without losing their value. People are so accustomed to the sight of a particular coin, that unless they be money dealers, they do not stop too curiously to inquire whether it is of the proper weight or not. In fact, when coins have been some time in use few persons know what their legal weight is. Many, for instance, do not associate the idea of a pound with any particular weight of Bullion : and thus, in the exchange for products and services, coins may pass at their nominal value long after they have lost much of their legal weight

As Posthumus says, in *Cymbeline*—

" 'Tween man and man they weigh not every stamp,
    Though light, take pieces for the figure's sake "

But when Coins are given in exchange for Bullion the case is different. The Value of Bullion is measured weight for weight with Coins. Consequently, if the Coins have lost their legal weight, a greater number of them must be given to purchase a given amount of Bullion than if they were of full weight. Thus, if the Mint Price of Silver is 5s. 2d. per ounce, that quantity of Coin ought by law to weigh an ounce : but if the coins have lost their legal weight, it is clear that *more* than 5s. 2d. must be given to buy an ounce of Bullion. It might, perhaps, take 6s., or even more, to buy an ounce of Bullion

The quantity of Coin at its full legal weight which is equal in weight to a given weight of Bullion, is called its **Mint Price** : but the quantity of the **Current** Coin which is actually equal to it in weight, is called the **Market Price** : and as, if the current coins have lost their weight, *more* of them must be given than if they are of full weight, the Market Price will apparently be higher than the Mint Price : and this is called a **Rise** *of the* **Market Price** *above the* **Mint Price**

Suppose that the Mint Price of Silver is 5s. 2d. per ounce: and the Market Price is 6s. per ounce : that means that 6s. weigh no more than 5s. 2d. ought to do : and, therefore, the current coinage is deficient about $\frac{1}{8}$ of its legal weight. Thus, in reality, it is clear that the rise of the Market Price is due to the **Depreciation** of the Coinage

Hence, we obtain this fundamental Law of the Coinage—

When the Market Price of Bullion rises above the Mint Price, the **Excess** *is the* **Proof** *and the* **Measure** *of the* **Depreciation** *of the Coinage*

In fact, the apparent rise of the Market Price of Bullion is due to exactly the same cause as has made the Mint Price of Silver apparently rise from £1 in the days of William the Conqueror to £3 2*s.* in the present day. It is merely that the weight of the current coins has been diminished

The Market Price of Bullion could never fall below the Mint Price, unless there were more Bullion in the Coin than there ought to be: and, in such a case the difference of the Market Price below the Mint Price would indicate the excess of the Coins above their legal weight

If a Change takes place in the Relative Value of the Gold and Silver Coins, to determine whether it is due to an Alteration in the Value of the two Metals or to a Depreciation of the Coinage

8. The considerations we have presented will enable us to solve a question of great practical importance. When both metals were used concurrently as Money, the Value of the Silver Coinage used to change with respect to the Gold. Thus guineas were originally coined to be of the value of 20*s.* in Silver : but in the reign of William III. guineas rose to 28*s.* and 30*s.* : and at the same time Silver Bullion rose from 5*s.* 2*d.* to 7*s.* an ounce

One party stoutly maintained that this was due to the scarcity of silver. This assertion was absurd on the face of it : because if silver had become very scarce as compared to gold, it is quite clear that silver would have *risen* as compared to gold and not *fallen*. That is, instead of guineas being worth 28*s.*, they would have been worth less than 20*s.* From the figures given above this assertion was self-contradictory : because as compared with gold, silver had apparently *fallen* in value, and as compared with silver it had apparently *risen* in value

But as the variation might proceed either from a *Diminution in Value* of Silver as compared to Gold : or from a *Depreciation* of the silver coinage, we are enabled to devise a test which will enable us to decide to which of these causes it was due

It is quite clear that a diminution in the Value of the coin cannot produce any difference between the Mint Price and the Market Price of Bullion : because by the very meaning of the term Mint Price, however plentiful or however scarce Silver may be, an ounce of it in Coin must always be of the exact weight or value of an ounce of it in Bullion

On the other hand, a *Depreciation* of the Coinage must inevitably produce a rise in the Market Price of Bullion above the Mint Price ; because, however scarce, or however plentiful, Bullion may be, three-quarters of an ounce of it in coin can never be equal in weight or value to an ounce of it in Bullion

The case may be shortly taken thus—Guineas may rise to 28*s.* in silver, either from a Diminution in Value of Silver : or from a Depreciation of the Silver Coinage. What is the test ? It is to be found in the Market Price of Silver. If the Silver Coinage is Depreciated, the Market Price will rise above the Mint Price : if it is a mere Alteration in the Value of Silver, it will not.

Evidently, however, both circumstances may take place. There may be an Alteration in the Value of the metals as well as a Depreciation of the Silver Coinage at the same time. And it is quite easy to devise a test in such a case : because the Depreciation of the Silver Coinage is measured by the difference between the Market and the Mint Price of Silver : and thus the Value of the Silver Coinage being rectified, it is quite easy to see whether it has changed in its relation to Gold

On Gresham's Law *of the* Coinage

9. We have now to notice a Law of fundamental importance in the Theory of the Coinage

Aristophanes first noticed the fact at Athens, that when a debased Coinage was issued along with a good Coinage, the good Coins all disappeared from circulation and the debased ones alone remained

This fact, which has been observed in all ages and countries, was long the puzzle of financiers and statesmen. Formerly, the Coinage of this country used to suffer very much from clipping and other bad practices. Repeated attempts were made to remedy the evil by issuing new coin from the Mint, without withdrawing the debased Coin. But all these efforts failed : the good coins invariably vanished from circulation, and the bad ones alone remained

At length Sir Thomas Gresham first explained the reason to Queen Elizabeth : and, therefore, we have called it " Gresham's Law of the Coinage:" and this name is now universally recognised

This Law was well expressed in an old pamphlet, thus—

" *When two sorts of Money are current in the same nation, of like Value by denomination, but not intrinsically, that which has the least Value will be current, and the other as much as possible hoarded,*" or exported

Which may be expressed shortly thus—

" *Bad money always drives good money out from circulation* "

The reason of this is plain. If full-weighted and depreciated coins are allowed to circulate together, one of two effects must necessarily follow. Either those persons who have commodities to sell will make a difference in their nominal price, according as they are paid in good or in light coin : that is, the light coin will be at a discount as compared to the good coin : or, if there be a law to prevent this, and to make both pass at the same nominal value, every one will endeavour to pay his debt at the least possible expense. He will always pay his debt in light coin

As values are always estimated by the weight of the metal, a law which declares that light coin shall be of the same value as good coin, is as great an anomaly as a law which declared that three are equal to four. But the consequence is very plain : if the law of this country declares that three ounces of silver shall be equal to four ounces, the possessors of the light coins always pay them away in preference to good ones; and Bullion dealers collect all the full weighted coins, and export them to foreign countries, where they pass at their full value. Thus the good coin quickly disappears from circulation, and the light coin alone remains.

Moreover, no one will bring Bullion to be converted into Coin. During the degraded state of the Silver coinage during the last century, the Market Price of Silver always exceeded the Mint price. Smith says that the Market Price of silver ranged from 5s. 4d. to 5s. 8d. an ounce before the re-coinage in 1774. And the second Report of the Lords' Committee of Secrecy in 1797 says—" But as the Mint Price of Silver Bullion has been, during the whole of the present century, considerably less than the market price of the precious metal, *the Silver Bullion imported could not be converted into Coin :* but having left a sufficient quantity for the use of our manufacturers, must have been again exported, and did not contribute in the smallest degree to augment the Coin of this kingdom "

The very same principle holds true even if the coin of both metals is full weighted, if the law attempts to fix a ratio between them which differs from the market rate of the world

In 1717, the Government having been sorely perplexed by the failure of all attempts to retain in circulation Gold and Silver coins, referred the whole matter to Newton, then Master of the Mint. Guineas nominally circulated at 21s. 6d. Newton showed that guineas were only worth 20s. 8d. according to the Market Value of Gold and Silver. Government advised the King to issue a proclamation making guineas current at 21s.

In consequence of attempting to make guineas current at 4d. above their Market Value, merchants universally agreed to make their bills payable in Gold : and Gold consequently then became the practical measure of value. All the good silver coins disappeared.

And for a similar but reverse reason, Silver became the recognised measure of value in France : because silver was rated in the Coinage higher than its Market Value

The same thing has been seen in France during the present century. About 1803 the legal relation between gold and silver was fixed at $15\frac{1}{2}$: and coins of gold and silver were struck at that ratio. But, in practice, coins of both metals were never really in general circulation together. Up to about 1856 silver was the general money in use. Twenty franc pieces in gold were very rarely seen : and, if any quantity were wanted, it was necessary to pay a premium, or *agio*

But, after 1856, when the great augmentation of gold took place, Gold drove Silver out of the country. Every steamer that left the ports was loaded with bags filled with five franc pieces, which departed like a flood. In fact, no country has ever yet succeeded in keeping gold and silver coins in unlimited circulation, when the coins were of full weight, at a ratio fixed by law

There can be no **Par of Exchange** *between countries which use* **Different** *Metals as their* **Legal Standard**

10. There can only be a real Par of Exchange between two countries when they both use the **same Metal** for their legal standard.

There can be no true Par of Exchange between countries which use *different* metals, such as Gold and Silver, as their Legal Standard. The relative Market Value of the two Metals is constantly varying, from causes entirely beyond the control of any law. It is no more possible to have a fixed price of one in terms of the other, than it is to have a fixed legal price of corn or of any other commodity

In 1797. when the Bank of England stopped payment, the House of Lords appointed a Committee to investigate the subject. The Committee, among other things, wished to ascertain the Par of Exchange between London and Hamburg : and they examined several merchants on the subject. But they were quite unable to agree among themselves what the true Par of Exchange between the two places was : and the Committee reported that they were unable to come to a satisfactory conclusion on the subject

There cannot, in the nature of things, be any fixed or true Par of Exchange between England and any country which uses a Silver Standard. It is only possible to say that such is the *usual Rate of Exchange* between them. Hence, when it is said that 25·21 francs is the Par of Exchange between England and France, it only means that such was reckoned as the usual Rate of Exchange between them, before the recent great disturbance in the relative value of the two metals. And even the best authorities differed in their estimate by several centimes. And between such countries it is sometimes impossible to decide certainly which way the Exchange is, unless the difference exceeds a certain amount

Effect of a Depreciated Coinage

11. Coins may circulate in their own country at their full nominal value, after they have lost a considerable amount of their weight by wear and tear, because persons in general are not very rigorous in weighing every Coin they receive

But when they are exchanged for Bullion, or for the Coins of a foreign country, they are always weighed and exchanged weight for weight. If, therefore, for any reason whatever, the English Coins have become degraded, worn, or clipped, and so lost their proper weight, they will evidently not buy so much Bullion, or full-weighted francs, as if they were of their full weight

If English sovereigns were in this depreciated state they might perhaps only purchase 24 francs instead of 25·21 francs. This would be called a **Fall** in the Foreign Exchanges

Or if an English merchant were obliged to pay a Debt of 2,521 francs in Paris, he would have to give more than £100 to purchase them. This would be called a **Rise** in the Foreign Exchanges : and the Exchange would be said to be so much **against** England by the amount of the difference

When English Coin is used to buy French Coins it may be looked at in two points of view—

1. A **Fixed** amount of English Coin may be used to buy an **Uncertain** amount of French Coin

2. An **Uncertain** amount of English coin may be required to buy a **Fixed** amount of French coin

In the first point of view a Fixed amount of Depreciated English Coin will buy a **Less** amount of French coin

In the second point of view it will require a **Greater** amount of depreciated English Coin to buy a Fixed amount of French Coin

Hence, when a Depreciated Coinage is said to produce a **Fall** *in the Foreign Exchanges, it means that a* **Given** *amount of English Coin will purchase a* **Less** *amount of Foreign Coin*

When a Depreciated Coinage is said to produce a **Rise** *in the Foreign Exchanges, it means that it requires a* **Greater** *Amount of English Coin to purchase a* **Fixed** *Amount of Foreign Coin*

A clear understanding of these expressions will prevent any confusion arising when they are used indiscriminately, as they often are, in discussions on the Exchanges. They are not contradictory as they might appear to be : they only refer to two different methods of estimating the Coinage

It is evident that this adverse state of the Exchanges will continue so long as the Depreciation of the Home Coinage exists : and that a restoration of the Home Coinage to its proper state will at once rectify the Exchanges

It is also evident that a Depreciation of the Coinage by a Debasement of its Purity will produce exactly the same effect

If the Coinage is in a **Depreciated** *State, to determine whether the* **Exchange** *is* **Favorable,** *at* **Par,** *or* **Adverse**

12. When the English Coinage is at its full legal weight £100 in sovereigns will purchase 2,521 French silver francs

Suppose that the Coinage becomes Depreciated so that the Market Price of Bullion rises to £4 3s.

Then the Market Price of £100 in full-weighted Coin is £106 11s. 7½d.

Suppose that the Exchange on Paris is at 23·80 : or that £100 of the current coin will purchase 2,380 francs : then £106 11s. 7½d. will purchase 2,536·63 francs

But, as the Par at the Mint Price is 2,521 francs, it is evident that the Difference between 2,521 and 2,536·63 francs is the extent to which the Real Exchange is in favor of England

It is also easy to see how much the Exchange is depressed. Because £100 ought to purchase 2536·63 francs, whereas they will only purchase 2,380 francs. Consequently the Exchange is depressed by 206·63 francs, or the 100 sovereigns are deficient in that amount of their legal weight : and this will be found to tally with the Rise of their Market Price above their Mint Price

Hence a Depreciated Coinage necessarily produces a **Rise** *of the Market Price of Bullion above the Mint Price : and a* **Fall** *in the Foreign Exchanges below Par*

Because it will require a Greater amount of the Current Coin to buy a Fixed amount of Bullion : and a Fixed amount of the Current Coin will buy Less amount of Foreign Coin

And evidently a Rise in the Market Price of Bullion above the Mint Price : and a Fall of the Foreign Exchanges below Par : **Proves** and **Measures** the **Depreciation** of the English Coinage

Hence, we have the following rules—

Find the Market Price of Bullion in London compared to the Mint Price

Multiply the Market Price so found by the Rate of Exchange

Then the Exchange is favorable, at Par, or Adverse, according as the result is Above, At, or Below Par

And the Depression of the Exchange, caused by the Depression of the Coinage, is the Difference between the Sum so expressed in the Mint and Market Prices, multiplied by the Rate of Exchange

In the excellent state in which our Coinage now is, the question of the Nominal Exchange is of little importance. But it is impossible to understand the history of the currency without it : and it is essential as regards all Foreign countries which use an Inconvertible and Depreciated Paper Money

On the Real or Commercial Exchange

13. We have now to explain the mechanism of the Real or Commercial Exchange

Suppose that A in London is Creditor to B, and Debtor to B', both in Edinburgh, in equal amounts

Then to settle these Debts it would be necessary for B in Edinburgh to send the money to A in London : and for A in London to send an equal amount of money to B' in Edinburgh. This would require two transmissions of money between London and Edinburgh at some expense

The business may be settled much more easily and cheaply if A in London sends B', his Creditor in Edinburgh, an Order upon B his Debtor. By this means both Debts are settled and discharged by B paying over to B' the money he owes A : that is, by the simple transfer of the money from B to B' in the same place :

instead of by two transmissions between London and Edinburgh. This order is termed a Bill of Exchange: and the operation is exactly similar to a person paying a Debt by a Cheque on his banker

Thus, an "Exchange," or a Delegation, requires at least *three* parties and *two* Debts

On an Exchange with Four Parties

14. The above is the simplest form of an Exchange. But the course of trade between two places gives rise to much more complicated transactions

In the above case A fulfils two characters or *personæ* : he is Creditor to one party and Debtor to another party in Edinburgh

But in the "Exchanges" it more usually happens that there are *four* parties

Suppose that A in London is Creditor to B in Edinburgh : and that B' in Edinburgh is Creditor to A' in London

Then to settle these Debts two transmissions of money are necessary between London and Edinburgh

But suppose that A' in London goes to A, and pays him the money he owes to B' in Edinburgh : and then buys from him the Debt which he has against B in Edinburgh. He then sends this order to his own Creditor, B', in Edinburgh : then B' presents the order to B : and receives from him the money he owes to A'. By this means both these Debts are settled by two local transfers in London and Edinburgh : and the expense of two transmissions of money between these places is saved

When all the Debts between London and London are exactly equal, they may all be paid and discharged by means of these "Exchanges," Delegations, or local transfers, without the use of any money

The Exchanges are then said to be at **Par**

On the **Time Par** *of* **Exchange**

15. Suppose, however, that the Debts between London and Edinburgh are not equal: and that Edinburgh wishes to send more money to London than it has to receive from London. Then the Demand for Bills is greater than the Supply

But, as it is cheaper to send a Bill than the cash, those who are bound to send Money will bid against each other for the Bills in the market, as for any other merchandise : and the Price of Bills will rise : or a **Premium** will have to be paid for a Bill on London

London is the great centre of Commerce : it is the seat of Government, to which the revenue is remitted from all parts of the country. The great families from all parts of the country go to reside there, and their revenues must be remitted to them there. Hence, there is always a much greater quantity of money seeking to flow to London from the country than the contrary. Consequently the Demand for Bills on London in the country is always greater than the Supply : and, therefore, Inland Bills on London are always at a premium

This premium is computed by **Time.** It is an essential part of the business of a banker to give these Bills. Within comparatively recent times a Bill on London at sight was charged 40 days' interest in Edinburgh. But since the introduction of railways this has been reduced to 4 days. If a person in Edinburgh now wants a Bill at sight on London he has to pay 1s. per cent., or four days' interest

This is termed the **Time Par** of Exchange between Edinburgh and London. There is a similar premium, or Time Par of Exchange, between all other towns in the country and London. This is termed **Inland Exchange**

It appears from this that when in any place the Demand for Bills on any other place is greater than the Supply, and, therefore, when *Bills rise to a premium*, the Exchanges are **adverse** to the first place, because it has more money to pay than to receive

But when the supply of Bills is greater than the Demand, the reverse takes place : *Bills fall to a Discount:* and the Exchanges are **favorable** to the first place, because it has more money **to** receive than to pay

It must be observed, however, that the interests of Buyers and Sellers of Bills are opposite : if the Exchange is unfavorable to buyers of Bills, or those who wish to send money it is equally favorable to the Sellers of Bills, or those who have to receive money

Buyers of Bills are also termed *Remitters:* and Sellers of Bills are also termed *Drawers*

On Foreign Exchange

16. The principle of Foreign Exchange is exactly the same as that of Inland Exchange. But there is very considerably more complication in the details, because different nations use different Metals as legal standards, and different Coinages

In Exchange between two foreign places and of different Moneys, the Money of one place is always taken as **Fixed**: and the Exchange is always reckoned in the **Variable** Quantity of the Money of the other place which is given for it

The former is termed the **Fixed** or **Certain** Price: and the latter the **Variable** or **Uncertain** Price

Moreover, the Foreign Exchanges are immensely complicated because every centre of Exchanges **Gives** the Variable Price to some places: and **Receives** the Variable Price from others

Between London and Paris the £ is the fixed price: and the Exchange is reckoned in the Variable sum of francs and centimes given for it

But on the contrary, between London and Spain the Dollar is the Fixed price: and the Exchange is reckoned in the Variable number of pence given for it

When any place is taken as the centre, if the Money of the place is the Fixed price, it is said to Receive the Variable price

But when the Money of the place is the Variable price; it is said to give the Variable price

Thus, London Receives from Paris so many francs and centimes for the £1: on the contrary, London gives to Spain so many pence for the Dollar

In the quotations of the Rates of Exchange it is usual to omit the Fixed price: and to state only the Variable price: and then that sum is termed the **Rate** *or* **Course** *of* **Exchange**

London **Receives** the Variable price from Amsterdam, Germany, France, Italy, Belgium, Switzerland, and Austria

London **gives** the Variable price to Lisbon, Spain, Gibraltar, St. Petersburg, Rio Janeiro, New York, and Calcutta

Effects of the Exchanges being **Favorable** *or* **Adverse** *to London*

17. As a General Rule, when the Exchanges are **Favorable** to London, Foreign Bills fall to a **Discount,** because London has more money to receive than to pay

When the Exchanges are **Adverse** to London, Foreign Bills rise to a **Premium,** because London has more money to receive than to pay. But, in consequence of the **Opposite** modes of reckoning the Exchanges in London on different countries, the very same effects will have to be expressed in **Opposite** terms, according as London **Receives** or **Gives** the Variable price

Exchange between London and Places **from** *which it* **Receives** *the Variable Price*

18. If the Exchange of London on Paris is favorable to London, and, therefore, the Supply of Bills is greater than the Demand, Bills fall to a Discount : and, consequently, the Rate of Exchange will rise above Par : that is, the £ will purchase **more** francs and cents. than the Par

But if the Exchange is Against London : the Demand for Bills will be greater than the Supply : and Bills will rise to a Premium : and, therefore, the £ will purchase **Fewer** francs and cents. : or the Exchange will fall below Par

And the same is true with respect to all other places from which London **Receives** the Variable price

Exchanges between London and Places **to** *which it* **Gives** *the Variable Price*

19. But, of course, the contrary takes place between London and all places *to which* it *Gives* the Variable Price

Thus, between London and Spain, when the Exchange is Favorable to London, she will give Fewer pence to buy the Dollar : or the Exchange will fall below Par

If the exchange between London and Spain is Against London, Bills rise to a premium, and London must Give more pence to buy the Dollar : or the Exchange will Rise above Par

And the same is manifestly true with respect to all places to which London Gives the Variable Price

Hence, when the Rate of Exchange between London and any other place varies from Par : in order to determine whether the Exchange is Favorable or Adverse, it is always necessary to consider whether London Gives the Variable Price to, or Receives the Variable Price from, that place

One reason of the complication of the subject of the Exchanges is that London *Gives* the Variable Price to some places and *Receives* it from others : consequently, the same Real state of the Exchanges requires opposite expressions in these opposite cases. But it is exactly the same with every centre of Exchanges : they each *Give* the Variable Price *to* some places, and *Receive* it *from* others

On the Limits of the Variations of the Exchanges

20.   When the Debts to be exchanged between any two places are exactly equal, the Demand and Supply of Bills at each place is exactly equal : and the Exchanges are at Par : because there is no money to be remitted from either side

But if one place has to send more money than it has to receive, the Demand for Bills will cause them to rise to a premium

It is the duty of the Debtor to place the money on the spot where the Debt is due, at his own risk and expense. Consequently as it is cheaper to send a Bill by post than to send the cash, with all the expenses of freight and insurance to pay : he would rather give a little more than the nominal value of the Bill in order to save the expense of sending the Specie

But he will not give more than the cost of sending the Specie : because if the price of the Bills were higher than that, it would be cheaper to send the Specie itself

Hence the cost of sending the Specie is a **Superior Limit** to the Variations of the Real Exchange

But the reverse case may also happen. The Supply of Bills in London on Paris may exceed the Demand.   In that case London has more money to receive than to pay. The Price of Bills will consequently fall below Par. But, for the same reason, the cost of transmitting Bullion will be an **Inferior Limit** below which the Price will not fall

Hence, the Limits of the Variations of the Exchanges are confined to **Twice** the cost of sending Specie between the two places

The Limits of the Variations of the Exchanges between two places are termed **Specie Points**: because, when the Rates of Exchange have a tendency to exceed them, Specie may be expected to flow in or out as the case may be

It must be observed, however, that these Limits of the Variations of the Exchange only apply to Bills payable at once : and to considerable periods. During short periods, and for Bills which have some time to run, the fluctuations of the Exchange may, from a variety of causes, greatly exceed these Limits

On Inconvertible Paper Money

21. The above considerations affect Coinages of Gold and Silver : but in modern times a new species of Money has come into use : and nearly every country has had recourse to it in times of public difficulty—and that is **Paper Money**

While Paper is convertible—*i.e.*, while the holder of it can compel the issuer to give Gold on demand for it—it is evident that it cannot circulate at a discount : because if it fell to a discount, the holders of it would at once go and demand Gold for it

In quiet and ordinary times a Bank can keep in circulation a very much larger amount of Notes or Bank Credits than the specie they are obliged to retain. As has been shown, banking profits can only be made by creating and issuing Credit in excess of specie. And so long as there is public confidence that the issuers can redeem this Credit on demand, the Credit circulates and produces, in all respects, identically the same effects as an equal amount of Gold

But, suppose that some great calamity happens, such as war, or an invasion, this confidence vanishes, and numerous persons would demand payment of their Credits in Gold

Under the circumstances, and with the enormous quantity of paper in circulation in modern times, every country in Europe has been obliged to suspend payments in cash: and to give an artificial value to the Paper by receiving it in payment for taxes, &c., at its nominal value in specie: and to make it Legal Tender.

When this is done the Paper Money becomes, in all respects, equivalent to a New Standard, just as much as Gold and Silver: and its Value is affected by exactly the same principles as affect the Value of Gold and Silver

Under the old system of attempting to fix the price of Gold relatively to Silver, there was no power of convertibility of one into the other, similar to the convertibility of the Bank Note. If silver fell to a discount, as compared with Gold, no one could demand, as a right, to have his silver exchanged for Gold. Consequently, the inevitable result of a considerable change in the Quantity or the Demand for either metal was a change in their relative values. In 1794, Gold rose to 84s., if purchased with *Silver* Bullion: but, if the Silver Coin had been convertible into Gold, like a Bank Note, this difference could never have arisen: any more than a Bank Note, convertible into Coin, can circulate at a discount as compared with Coin

Now, Paper Money, when issued as a substantive Coinage, follows exactly the same rules. If only the usual Quantity of it be issued, *i.e., no greater Quantity than would have been issued if it had been convertible into Coin*, it will continue to circulate at its Par value. But if these issues be increased in quantity, and if the natural corrective of excessive issues be taken away, namely—payment in cash on demand, exactly the same result follows as attends a greatly increased quantity of Silver, and it falls to a Discount

Lord King's Law *of* Paper Money

22. When either of two metals used as Coinage becomes greatly increased in quantity it becomes Diminished in Value, as compared with the other: and if Gold and Silver, not being convertible, are compelled to circulate at a fixed ratio, in virtue of Gresham's Law, the one which is underrated invariably disappears from circulation, and is exported to foreign countries, where it may exchange for its true value

When one metal Diminishes in Value with respect to the other, it is not *Depreciation*, because it has a Value of its own in the market of the world. But when Paper Money is used which has no value of its own, but merely an artificial value, and it becomes excessive in quantity, it cannot be exported : because it has only a local value, and not a general value in the market of the world. It falls to a discount as compared with Coin : and in this case it is **Depreciation** : because it professes to be equal in value to Coin, and it is not so

If it is attempted to maintain a fixed ratio between Paper Money and Coin after the Paper has fallen to a discount, exactly the same result follows as takes place when Coin of inferior value is attempted to be made to circulate at par with Coin of superior value. The Coin is all hoarded or exported : it entirely disappears from Circulation : and nothing but Paper remains. As the quantity of Paper increases it falls in value : all Prices rise : the Foreign Exchanges fall : and all the Foreign Trade of the country is deranged

A few years after the Bank of England suspended Cash Payments in 1797, the Price of Bullion rose and the Foreign Exchanges fell : deranging the whole course of the Foreign Trade. Some able writers, the most conspicuous of whom was Lord King, maintained that this was due to the Depreciation of the Bank Note. Strong interests, however, contested this doctrine. The Bank contested it, because it found it profitable to issue as much Paper as possible : merchants contested it because they were afraid that their accommodation would be restricted. After a short time the value of the Bank Note improved, and the question slumbered

In 1809 the same phenomena recurred in a much more aggravated form, and gave rise to the appointment of the celebrated Bullion Committee. All the witnesses before this Committee except one maintained that it was not the Bank Note which had fallen, but that Gold had risen

The Report, however, drawn up by Huskisson, Horner, and Thornton entirely disproved this assertion, and showed that the Rise of the Market Price of Gold and the Fall of the Foreign Exchanges was due entirely to the Depreciation of the Bank

Note from Excessive quantity: and it recommended a Diminution of its Issues: so as to restore the Value of the Bank Note

Resolutions in accordance with the Report were moved by Horner: it was proved that there were two prices in common use: a Paper Price and a Money Price: and that a £1 Bank Note and 7s. were commonly given for a guinea. Nevertheless, under the influence of party passion the House of Commons voted that a guinea was equal to a £1 Bank Note and 1s. in public estimation: or that 27 = 21. Freed by this vote from all control, the Bank made more extravagant issues than ever: so that in 1815 the Bank Note was only equal to 14s. 6d.

However, the doctrines of the Bullion Report gradually convinced the Mercantile world: and, in 1819, they were almost unanimously in their favor

Lord King's Law of Paper Money is this—

A Rise of the Paper or Market Price of Bullion above the Mint Price: and a Fall of the Foreign Exchanges below the Limits of the Real Exchange: is the Proof and the Measure of the Depreciation of the Paper Money

This principle is so universally admitted now, and so perfectly evident, that there is no use in wasting more words to prove it

It shows that Paper Money must always be restrained within certain Limits to maintain a Par Value with Gold. But if this be duly done, a certain amount of Inconvertible Paper Money may circulate along with specie at Par

If the Bank of England had taken proper measures for controling and limiting its issues, its Notes might have circulated at Par with Gold. In 1874 the Inconvertible Notes of the Bank of France circulated at Par with Coin, because they were carefully limited

The doctrines of the Bullion Report lay down the principles by which all Credit and Paper Currency, whether Convertible or Inconvertible, must be regulated—namely, a strict attention to the Price of Bullion, and the state of the Foreign Exchanges

The demonstration of the Bullion Committee was, in course of time, universally accepted by the Banking and Mercantile world: the only difficulty left unsolved was the Practical Measures to be adopted to carry it into effect

However, after several unsuccessful attempts to discover the true method of giving effect to this doctrine, this problem has now been successfully solved : and thus the Theory of the Paper Currency is now complete

Effect *of the* Restoration *of the* Coinage *on the* Exchanges

23.   In the preceding remarks on the Nominal Exchange it has been shown that the depreciation or degradation of the Coin in which the Exchanges are reckoned must necessarily derange all the Exchanges of the country : and that a Restoration of the Coin to its due legal state will be sufficient to rectify the Exchanges

But the state of any other portion of the Currency, or Circulating Medium, than the one in which the Exchanges are reckoned, will not affect them

In the early part of the reign of William III., the Silver Coinage in which the Exchanges were then reckoned had fallen into a most disgraceful state from clipping, and other causes. On collecting bags of coin from different parts of the country it was found that their weight scarcely exceeded by one half what it ought to have been. The Exchanges were entirely disordered, and the Commerce of the country was thrown into utter confusion. In the beginning of 1696 the great work of the Restoration of the Coinage was begun, and by July the new Coin began to be issued in considerable quantities, and the Exchanges were immediately rectified

Bank of England Notes at this period were at a heavy discount : because the Bank had suspended payments in cash : but that produced no effect on the Exchanges, because they were not reckoned in Bank Notes, but exclusively in Silver Coin

On Exchange Operations

24.   Exchange operations consist in buying, selling, importing, and exporting **Bullion** : termed "**Bullion** operations " : and buying and selling Bills : termed " **Banking** operations "

The object of our present remarks is to explain the general causes which produce those movements of Bullion, which so sorely vex the banking and commercial world

I 2

Exchange operations of both sorts may be either direct or indirect : that is, they may take place directly between the two places : or the final operations may be effected through the medium of one or more intermediate countries

It has been shown that for Bills payable at sight, or as they are now coming to be called Cheques, the limits of the variations of the Exchanges cannot exceed twice the cost of transmitting Bullion, which are called the Specie points : because when they are reached, Bullion may be expected to flow in or out

When the Bills, however, have a considerable time, such as three months or more to run before they are payable ; causes may operate which may produce *temporary* fluctuations of the Exchanges considerably beyond these limits

These causes are chiefly—

1. The necessity that the holders of the Bills may have to realise them, even at a considerable sacrifice to maintain their own position

2. The doubtful position of the acceptors, or the general discredit of the place they are drawn upon

3. The differing relative Values of the precious Metals, which are the standard of payment at each place

4. The respective Rates of Discount at each place

Now it may often be that from these combined causes it may be considerably more profitable to possess Bullion at one place than another. Exchange operators, then, export Bullion from one place to another for the sake of the profit. They create Bills upon such a place : they draw Bills upon their correspondents : discount their Bills : and remit the proceeds to meet their Bills when due

It used to be the dogma of the mercantile world that Bullion is only exported to liquidate a previous state of indebtedness : and that consequently an export of Bullion comes to a natural end, when the indebtedness is discharged. But this is a most grievous error. The sufficient difference in the profit of possessing Bullion at two places, causes operators to **Fabricate** Bills for the express purpose of exporting Bullion, without any previous indebtedness : and, of course, this drain will not cease so long as this possibility of profit exists. The only effectual way of annihilating this profit, and causing the drain to cease, is by **Raising the Rate of Discount**

Between countries in which there are no restraints on trade, the Exchanges will never vary much except on some sudden emergency. But there are countries with which, owing to their prohibitive laws, the Exchanges are permanently unfavorable: because they will take nothing but Bullion for their commodities. Russia is one of these countries: and hence if not modified by other circumstances, Bills upon Russia would always be at a premium. But here again the effect of trafficking steps in, which always has a tendency to equalise prices. The merchant who deals in Bills acts upon the same principles as the dealer in any other commodities: he buys them where they are cheapest, and sells them where they are dearest. Hence he will try to buy up Russian Bills on other Exchanges, or Debt markets, where they are cheaper and sell them on the London Debt Market, where they are dearer.

On the other hand, from the course of trade between England and Italy, the Debt which Italy owes to England is usually greater than the contrary: hence Italian bills will usually be at a discount, or cheap in the London Debt Market. So the Bill merchant buys them up cheap here, and sends them to some other market—Paris for instance—where they may be at a premium

By these means the price of Bills is raised where they are cheapest and lowered where they are dearest. The general result will be to melt all the differences between separate countries into one general result: so that the Exchanges will not be favorable with some countries and adverse with others: but they will be generally favorable or adverse with all the rest of the world

On the Arbitration of Exchange

25. Supposing however a merchant has to remit money to Paris, while the Exchange with Paris is unfavorable to England, he may possibly discover a more advantageous way of remitting it than by buying a Bill on Paris directly. Thus for instance while Bills on Paris are at a premium in London, those on Hamburg might be at a discount: and Bills on Paris might be at a discount in Hamburg

So if the merchant buys a Bill on Hamburg, and sells it to his agent there, and directs him to purchase a Bill on Paris with the proceeds, he may be able to discharge his Debt in Paris at a less sum than he would have to pay for a Bill on Paris in London

This circuitous way of settling his Debt involves additional charges for brokerage, commission, postage, &c.: but the effect of it is still further to equalise the Exchanges between London and all other countries. This circuitous method is called the **Arbitration of Exchanges**: and the sum which is given in London for the ultimate price it realises in Paris is called its *Arbitrated Price*. When only three places are used in the operation, it is called *Simple Arbitration*. When more than three are employed it is called *Compound Arbitration*. It is evident that the quicker and cheaper the communication between countries becomes, the less room will there be for such operations, because the limits of the variations of the real Exchanges, which are the margin which renders such operations possible, will constantly diminish

The scale on which these indirect operations of Exchange are carried on is immense. There is no Exchange between places to and from which remittances have not constantly to be made. Consequently when such places trade, their accounts must be settled by means of Bills on some recognised centre. London is the banking centre of the world. From the enormous exports of England to all quarters of the globe, remittances have to be made to London from every part of the world. There is therefore a constant demand for Bills upon London to discharge the debts incurred for these commodities. Hence although the exporters may send their goods to different countries: yet if they can draw upon London, their Bills will be sure to find some purchasers somewhere to be remitted to London. Hence Bills upon London bear a higher price, and meet with a readier sale than those upon other places

One country A may import from B less than she exports: consequently a Debt is due from A to B. Also B exports to another country C, more that she imports: consequently a Debt is due from C to B: and A may discharge its Debt to B, by ransferring to it its claim against C

As many countries trade with one another between which there is no Exchange, their claims are mutually adjusted by Bills upon London the great banking centre. Hence the London Exchange is the most important in the world, and requires the greatest attention to be paid to it

On the Import and Export of Bullion

26. We must now consider the causes which affect the import and export of Bullion

As the British Ilands do not produce the precious metals to any extent worth considering, they are only to be obtained in this country by importation : and we must now consider the various sources from which they come, and the different causes which produce an influx or efflux of them. They are to be treated in every respect like any other foreign commodity : and are obtained by the same means as any other that we require for domestic consumption, which is not a native product

The trade in Bullion may be divided into two distinct branches : the one where it is carried on directly with the countries in which gold and silver are native products : and the other with those countries which do not produce it : but which, like our own, have no means of supplying themselves with it except by foreign commerce

I. With Bullion-producing countries

Before the discoveries in California and Australia, the chief Bullion-producing countries were Mexico and Peru. There were others it is true, but we need not specify them, because the same principle applies to them all : and to describe them all would rather belong to a work on commerce generally

British merchants have establishments, or correspondents in those countries, to whom they consign their goods, and their agents exchange them for Bullion brought down by the natives, and which is collected in large quantities : and in former times used to be brought home in ships of war for the sake of security

In those countries Bullion is treated exactly like any other commodity, such as tea, wool, or wine : and the British goods of all kinds are exported to them for the express purpose of being exchanged for Bullion to be remitted home

The limits to this exportation are precisely similar to the limits of the exportation of any other commodities. It is clear that by the time the Bullion reaches this country, it ought to be sufficient to cover the original price of the goods, and all charges on them on their way out : as well as the agent's commission there : the charges for freight : insurance, and commission for bringing it home : and a fair mercantile profit over and above all these expenses. Unless it does that the commerce is not profitable. If too many goods are exported to those Bullion-producing countries their exchangeable relation with Bullion falls ; and they will not purchase a sufficient quantity of Bullion to afford this profit : and the further export of goods to these places must cease until the goods first sent out are consumed, and fresh ones required at such a price as to afford a profit. The purchase of Bullion then in these countries is a very simple affair and requires no further notice

II. *With Countries which do not produce Bullion*

The causes which cause an influx or efflux of Bullion between this and other countries which do not produce it are vastly more intricate, and have excited long and keen controversies

Taking this country as the centre, the transmission of Bullion to or from it is influenced by the **Seven** following causes—

1. The Balance of Payments to be made to or by it
2. The State of the Foreign Exchanges
3. The State of the Currency
4. By the Remittances made to this country as the Mercantile centre of the world, to meet payments due to other countries
5. By the Political Security of this and other countries
6. By the State of the Money Market : or the comparative Rates of Discount in this and neighbouring countries
7. By the free or prohibitive Tariffs of this and other countries, as they permit or forbid our manufactures to be imported into them

There are, then, **Seven** different causes which act upon the movements of Bullion : and as all these causes may be acting in all sorts of different ways, either in conjunction or opposition to each other, it is evident that the Foreign Exchanges is one of the most intricate branches of human knowledge. The inveterate error of mercantile opinion for a long time was that there is only one cause of an export of Bullion, namely a balance of mercantile indebtedness to be discharged

On Commercial Operations

27. For many centuries it was held that Money alone is wealth : and it was considered the true policy of every country to encourage by every means in its power the import of Bullion, and to discourage its export : and most if not all of the European nations have gone so far, at one time or another, as to prohibit its export by law. The profit of foreign commerce was estimated solely by the quantity of gold and silver it brought into the country : and the Theory of Commerce seemed to be reduced to a general scramble among all nations to try which could draw to itself most gold and silver from others

According to this theory the gain of one party was the loss of another : every article produced in one country and imported into another was held to be a direct loss to the importing country. This was what was called the Mercantile system

According to this theory, the leading maxim which governed the Legislature was to make the exports exceed the imports : and the conclusion drawn was that the difference, or balance, must be paid for in cash by the debtor nation. When two nations traded with one another the excess of the exports above the imports was called the " Balance of Trade." And the nation was supposed to gain exactly the excess of the exports over the imports, and to lose the excess of the imports, above the exports

This theory having been believed in for centuries, and having been the cause of innumerable commercial wars, was seen to be fallacious about the beginning of the eighteenth century, and was finally exploded by the Economists

The admirable chapter of Adam Smith on the Mercantile system is a masterly exposure of the fallacy of the theory, and is, certainly, one of the soundest and best written in his whole work, from the more than usual consistency of its ideas, and the lucidity of its style.   Most persons whose knowledge of Economics does not extend beyond Smith, suppose that he was the first person to demonstrate its fallacy.   This, however, is a complete error. Its fallacy was perceived and acknowledged more than half a century before his day

So far from the principle of the Mercantile system being true that gold and silver are the most profitable and desirable articles of import, the direct reverse is unquestionably true, that gold and silver are, of all objects of commerce, the most unprofitable : and it is a certain maxim of commerce in a state of freedom that Bullion will not be imported until it has become unprofitable to import any other article.   There is no class of traders who derive so little profit, in proportion to the Capital invested in their business, as dealers in Bullion and Money of all sorts, whether they be Bullion merchants or Bankers

On *the* Balance *of* Trade

28.   There is no expression in commerce more common than the "Balance of Trade," and it may be as well to give the interpretation of it generally received during the last century, and which is not yet wholly extinguished

Mr. Irving, Inspector-General of Imports and Exports in 1797, defined it thus—"The common mode of considering that question has been to set off the value of the imports as stated in the public accounts against the value of the exports : and the difference between the one and the other has been considered the measure of the increase or decrease of the national profit"

And Mr. Hoare, a banker of eminence for twenty-two years, said—" I consider the only proper means of bringing gold and silver into this country to arise from the surplus of our exports over our imports, and that ratio or proportion which is not imported in goods must be paid for in Bullion. In the year 1796 the imports of this country appeared to be £19,788,923, and the exports appear to be £33,454,583, which ought to have brought to this country Bullion to the amount of the difference, or £13,665,660 "

We have made these extracts because they convey in the fewest words possible the whole ideas on the subject, and they were made by persons of great commercial eminence before the Committee of the House of Commons. Mr. Irving, indeed, said that to apply this principle to the whole trade of the country would be highly erroneous. We therefore do not cite him as approving the theory, but only stating distinctly what it was. But Mr. Hoare, a banker of eminence and long experience, adopted it. And we believe that this theory of the Balance of Trade is still believed by many persons. Nevertheless, there never existed a more complete chimera and pernicious delusion than this said doctrine of the Balance of Trade, nor one which has exercised a more disastrous influence on commercial legislation

We will now take an example of the simplest description of trading to show the folly of the old doctrine of the Balance of Trade, as that will illustrate the principle as well as the most elaborate

When our ships traded to the South Seas they took out with them axes, beads, and other trifles which were of very little value in this country, and bartered them for all sorts of curiosities, shells, &c., which were very valuable in England

A pair of fine shells from the South Seas in many cases is worth ten guineas in England which an English sailor obtained perhaps in exchange for an axe worth 2s. 6d. The English sailors thought the natives very simple to give away such valuable curiosities for such common things. The natives doubtless had the same opinion of the English sailors. They thought them very simple to give away such valuable things as axes, beads, &c., for so common things as a few shells

Each party, however, exchanged what was common and cheap in his own country for what was scarce and valuable. The axes were many times more valuable in Fiji than the shells : the shells were many times more valuable in London than the axes. Thus an English sailor by giving away what was perhaps worth 2s. 6d. obtained in exchange what was worth ten guineas : and the difference was his profit. Thus both parties gained by the exchange. The shells were worth many axes in London : the axes were worth many shells in Fiji : and this is the genuine spirit of commerce

This simple transaction is a type of all commerce. The value of the shells in London arises from the desire of the people to possess them and their scarcity. The value of the axes in Fiji arises from the desire of the people to possess them and their scarcity. The colored beads were just as valuable to the untutored savages as precious stones to civilised Europeans. The commerce of all nations is exactly the same in principle as that between the sailors and the savages. It all consists in exchanging what is common and cheap for what is scarce and dear in them reciprocally. And of course both parties must gain by the very nature of the transactions

But according to the old doctrine of the Balance of Trade, England, having exported goods of the value of 2s. 6d., and imported goods to the value of ten guineas, owed the balance which required to be paid in gold

Thus the very reverse of the old doctrine of the Balance of Trade is true. So long as the goods imported are the payment for the goods exported it is clear that the profit to England is exactly the value of the goods imported above that of the goods exported. And as all the expenses of conveying the exports to the foreign country and of bringing the imports from the foreign country must be defrayed out of this difference, and in addition there must be the merchant's profit, it is evident that there must be a very considerable excess of the value of the imports above that of the exports if the commerce is to be carried on at a profit.

But it would be a great mistake to suppose that all the imports are the payments for the exports

The goods imported, and which are entered in the returns of the Custom House, form different classes. (1) They are the payment for goods exported : (2) They are goods sent here for sale or speculation : (3) They are goods sent here to be bonded, and re-exported to other countries

But as the Custom House returns do not discriminate between these classes of imports, it is evident that no means exist of ascertaining the respective quantities of the imports which belong to each class : and consequently it is absolutely impossible to determine whether the exchanges are favorable or adverse, from the mere Custom House returns

The Exchanges are then an inscrutable mystery even while confined to the Custom House returns. But at the present time they are rendered still more inscrutable, because in recent times a new article of import and export between countries has come into existence, viz., **Securities** of all sorts. Bills of Exchange, Government Securities, and securities of private companies of all sorts, are now imported and exported between countries exactly like material merchandise, and they have exactly the same effects on the Exchanges as material goods. But as all these Securities pass through the Post Office and not through the Custom House, there is of course no means of ascertaining their amount

The Foreign Exchanges are then an inscrutable mystery so far as regards any returns which are procurable. They can only be judged of by the actual demand for specie, either for export or import that may exist at any moment which arises from causes which are absolutely impenetrable to any inquirer

Simple Examples of Commercial Operations

29. We shall now give a few examples of simple commercial operations to illustrate certain general principles. To give a complete exposition of the foreign exchanges, one of the most complicated branches of human knowledge, would require a large treatise

Suppose a merchant in London sends out £1,000 of goods to Bordeaux. By the time they arrive there the mere addition of freight, insurance and other charges will probably have increased their cost of production, or the cost of placing them in the market there to £1,050, supposing them to be sold without any profit at all.   But as the merchant would never have sent them to that market unless he expected to realise a good profit, we may suppose that they sell for £1,200

His correspondent at Bordeaux instead of remitting the money to England would find it more profitable to invest the proceeds of the goods in some native product which would fetch a good price in England.   The chief native product of that country is *wine*: so the agent, after deducting all charges, would invest the proceeds in wine, and send it to England in payment of the goods.   If the markets were favorable this wine might be sold for £1,500 in England : and after deducting all charges on the cargoes both ways, the difference would be the merchant's profit. In this case no specie would pass between the countries.   The merchant would import more than he had exported : and his profits are the excess of the value of the inward cargo above that of the outward cargo, after deducting all charges both ways

The merchant's agent at Bordeaux would have to consider the state of the market both at Bordeaux and London, before he could determine whether he should send specie or wine in payment of the goods.   Supposing that the goods are sold at a good profit at Bordeaux, he must consider the price of the wine both at Bordeaux and in London.   From various circumstances the price of the wine at Bordeaux might be very high, and from various circumstances the price of the wine in London might be very low ; so that if he were to send wine, it might result in a loss.   If there were no other native product than wine he would have to remit specie, and then the exchange would be in favor of London.   But before the merchant in London could reckon his profits, he would have to deduct the charges on the specie

Whether the transaction was profitable or not to the merchant would entirely depend on the amount of specie he received for his goods after deducting all charges.   If there was a scarcity of such goods at Bordeaux he might realise good profits : but it would be very improbable that he would realise as high profits on the single operation, as in the double one of exporting goods and importing wine. The import of the specie would therefore be less profitable to him and to the nation at large than the import of the wine

The reasons which caused the export of specie from Bordeaux were the scarcity and dearness of wine at Bordeaux and its abundance and cheapness in London. Hence we gather that the scarcity and dearness of native products is a sure cause of the export of specie from a country: on the contrary an abundant supply of cheap products of all kinds both native and foreign will cause an importation of Bullion

The Exchange being in favor of a country means nothing more than that, from whatever causes, Bullion has to be remitted to it. But the above example is as good as a thousand, to show the dangerous fallacy of drawing any conclusion as to the advantage of the trade to England, from the simple fact of the Exchange being favorable, and an influx of specie taking place.

If Bordeaux had but one native product—wine—the chance of finding the markets both at Bordeaux and London favorable for importing produce instead of specie would be limited to that single article. But if it had other products the chances would be increased of finding articles to suit the respective markets : and the chances would evidently be multiplied according to the numbers and variety of its products. ·Hence we see the immense importance of making London the entrepot for all the products of the world, so as to multiply the chances of being able to pay for our imports by exports of products rather than in specie

The example given above is of the simplest description, and a merchant of eminence, who has correspondents in different parts of the world might easily multiply these operations so as to visit many markets before the returns of his cargo were brought home. Thus instead of having the wine sent home from Bordeaux, his correspondent might find it more profitable to send it to Buenos Ayres, and dispose of it there. One chief native product there is hides : and we may suppose that his correspondent there might invest the proceeds of the cargo of wine in hides : which there might be a favorable opportunity of selling in the West Indies. When the cargo arrives in the West Indies, instead of remitting the proceeds directly home, it might happen that, owing to a scarcity of corn at home, it might be very high there, and cheap in Canada : so he would invest the proceeds of the hides in sugar: despatch the sugar to Canada, where the merchant's correspondent there would dispose of it, and purchase corn, which he would send to England

In this case there are five distinct operations : and as there may be a profit upon each of them, by the time the ultimate returns of the goods which originally cost £1,000 are brought to England, it may be that the profit very far exceeds the original outlay : and no specie has been sent from one country to another in the whole course of the extended operations

We may now take New York as the starting place. The staple products of America are bread stuffs and provisions. A merchant of New York sends a cargo of corn to Liverpool, and his correspondent there will endeavour to invest the proceeds of that in British goods, if he finds that the state of the markets in England and New York will make such an operation profitable. If the price of corn is very high here, and the price of goods is also very high here and low in New York, it is clear that nothing but specie will be sent. When a great and unexpected dearth of corn occurs in England, and its price rises enormously high, which, however, can never happen again, the infallible result is to cause a great drain of specie for the time being, because our necessity for corn is much more pressing and immediate than their demand for goods. The only way to arrest such a drain of specie is to effect such a reduction in the price of our goods so as to make it more profitable to export goods than specie. It was one of the objects of the Bank Act of 1844 to enforce such a contraction of credit at such times as would reduce the price of goods, so as to make it possible to send them instead of specie

In the cases we have hitherto been considering, we have described the operations as if merchants were left perfectly free to carry the goods whither they pleased, and were not met and obstructed by artificial obstacles purposely devised for interfering with their business, by the laws of different nations. But all modern nations, and our own among the rest, have habitually discouraged the importation of foreign goods, and imposed heavy duties for the specific purpose of excluding them, as they conceived the extraordinary idea that all foreign goods brought into a country are so much loss to it

Thus the statute of William III., 1688, c. 24, says—" It hath been found by long experience that the importing of French commodities of all sorts have much exhausted the treasure of this nation, lessened the value of the native commodities and manufactures thereof, and greatly *impoverished* the English artificers and handicrafts, and caused great *detriment* to the Kingdom in general."

If we consider the effect of these prohibitory laws in one place it will equally apply to every other. Thus, suppose that there are high protecting duties at Bordeaux against British goods : as the customer must ultimately pay all the expenses and charges on the goods, it will have the effect of greatly raising the market price there, and diminishing the number of persons who can afford to buy them : and hence as the market is contracted, a smaller quantity of goods will overstock it than if it were more extended. This will cause a less quantity of goods to be sent from England, and it will cause a larger proportion of specie to be remitted to pay for the products of Bordeaux

This example shows that the inevitable effect of high protecting duties between country and country is to cause a much more frequent transmission of specie from one to the other than would be the case in an unfettered state of commerce : unless indeed the smuggler steps in, who is the natural corrector of this commercial insanity

The effect then of prohibitive duties is to cause an influx of specie : but it must not be supposed that this is a favorable sign, as it is certainly the least profitable import a merchant can receive for his goods. And there is this very marked difference between an influx of specie under the Protectionist system, and under a Free Trade system, that the former is accompanied by a great dearth of foreign commodities, but the latter is an infallible sign of a great abundance of them : as specie is never imported when men are allowed to follow their own interests, until our markets are already so overstocked with commodities that it has ceased to be profitable to import more

K

The foregoing cases convey a simple general outline of the course of trade between countries ; and we gather from them the following results respecting the influx or efflux of specie

I.   The cause of specie being imported is when the price of goods is so low in England and so high in foreign countries as to tempt foreigners to send here to buy goods : or to induce our merchants to export them to foreign countries

II.   The cause of specie being exported from England is that there is some great and pressing demand for some commodity, in this country, as formerly for corn in the failure of the harvest, or other food of the people, and other commodities are so scarce and dear that they cannot be exported with a profit : or that the commodity is wanted in such vast quantities, that the foreigners cannot consume our goods which we should prefer to send in payment for them fast enough : so that specie must be sent : and the greater the difference in price the greater will be the drain of specie : or that other markets are already so overstocked with our goods, which are depressed below their usual market value there

This is what is meant by overtrading : and from this circumstance we see that *overtrading is a sure cause of a drain of specie from this country*

The failure of the cereal crops in this country used to be another sure cause of a drain of specie.   But with the countries of the world now ready to pour in their supplies in the event of a deficient harvest, we may expect that corn will never again rise to a famine price in this country.   The great commercial crisis of 1847 was caused by several years of overtrading, and the failure of the potato crops in Ireland and the cereal harvests in Great Britain.   We shall have hereafter to examine the policy and the effects of the Bank Act of 1844 in meeting it

There are some countries from which we draw articles of prime necessity, but to which, from different circumstances, we do not remit goods in payment.   Russia was the great source of our supply of hemp, tallow, and flax : and we used to import these products to the value of £12,000,000 yearly : but from the prohibitive nature of her tariff, we were unable to send over our products in payment of these goods to anything like a similar amount in value. To such a country the difference must be remitted in specie, to the mutual loss of both parties : and unless there were other means of equalising the exchanges, the exchange with Russia would always be unfavorable

The chief export trade of Ireland to England was in articles of food—pigs, cattle, oats, butter, eggs. Great quantities of these came from Ireland, but as these were entirely devoted to pay the extravagant rents which the Irish landlords used to screw out of their unfortunate tenants, who had nothing over after they had paid their rents, they were unable to consume any English goods in exchange for those they exported. In consequence of this, their value had to be remitted in specie : and thus the exchange between England and Ireland used to be almost uniformly in favor of Ireland. If Ireland had been sufficiently wealthy to have consumed English goods instead of being paid in specie, it would have been far more advantageous for both parties : for English industry would have been promoted, and Ireland would have gained more valuable imports

These two examples illustrate what we said before, that the frequent transmission of specie between countries which do not produce it, indicates a less profitable trade than the exchange of products

If, then, specie be coming in from a country, it shows that we have already got so many of their products that it will not pay to import any more : and if specie be going out to a country, it shows that we have already sent out so many goods to that country that it will not pay to send any more

Now, suppose commerce to be in that desirable and healthy state in which no specie passes between non-bullion-producing countries, who could tell which way the balance of trade inclined ? Each country would show a favorable balance, taking the imports and the exports at their market prices in each country

Each country would show that their imports exceeded their exports : that is, each would show that they had gained by their commerce : for the very simple reason that the value of the imports in their own market would be greater than the value of the exports : and unless it was so it is manifest trade could not be

K 2

carried on : because all the expenses and profits of trade are provided for by the difference between the value of the exports and the value of the imports. Hence, unless both parties gain by the transaction, commerce could not be carried on

The fundamental fallacy about the Balance of Trade which seems to have taken possession of the Legislature was that the interests of individuals were opposed to those of the State. They seemed to think that every merchant had entered into a conspiracy to ruin the State, which he tried to carry into effect by becoming as prosperous himself as he could. They missed the obvious truism that the prosperity of the State is made up of the prosperity of the individuals composing it : and that every one is far keener in discerning what conduces to his own prosperity than the State can be : and that if private merchants found it to their advantage to import products rather than specie, it could not be advantageous to the State to force trade in a contrary direction

On the **Rate of Discount** *as influencing the Exchanges*

30. We have now to treat of a cause of the movements of Bullion which has acquired an importance in modern times far exceeding what it ever did before: namely, a difference in the **Rate** *of* **Interest** or **Discount** between two countries

In former times, when the communication between different places was slow and expensive, before the days of railroads and steamers, a considerable difference might exist between the Rates of Discount in two places, without causing any movement of Bullion from one place to the other

But that is not possible now. Communication between places is now so rapid and inexpensive, that directly the Rate of Discount in two places differs by more than the cost of sending Bullion from one to the other, an immediate flow of Bullion commences from one to the other

This is in exact accordance with the usual mercantile principle that operates in every other case, that if the difference of price of the same article in any two markets exceeds the cost of sending it from one to the other, it will immediately be sent : and this movement will continue so long as the difference in the price continues

Now, let us take an extreme case to illustrate the principle. Suppose that the Rate of Discount in London was 2 per cent., and in Paris 10 per cent.

That would mean that a merchant could sell a debt of £100 for £98 in London, and only for £92 in Paris. But the expense of sending bullion from London to Paris now is not more than ½ per cent.

The consequence of this would be that foreign merchants would send their Bills over in shoals to London to be discounted : and they would take away the specie

Not only that, but Bullion dealers in England would fabricate Bills for the express purpose of having them discounted, and exporting the specie

Bullion dealers trade in Bullion, just as other merchants trade in goods : and if they see that they can buy Gold at 2 per cent. in London, and sell it at 10 per cent. in Paris: they of course will do so. And it is evident that this drain will not cease until the Price of Gold is so far equalised between the two places as to destroy this profit

Consequently at the present day it is the imperative duty of the Bank of England to keep a steady watch on the Rates of Discount in neighbouring countries, and to follow their variations so as to prevent it being profitable to export Bullion from this country

On **Foreign Loans, Securities,** *and* **Remittances,** *as affecting the Exchanges*

31. Besides the state of national indebtedness arising out of Commercial operations, other causes may affect the Exchanges

Formerly during foreign wars England being more abundant in money and material resources than in men, used to subsidise foreign powers to a considerable amount : and the method of transmitting such a loan to the best advantage to the remitting country was an operation of considerable nicety and delicacy. To withdraw a very large amount of actual coin at any given time from a commercial country might produce the most disastrous consequences when so many engagements had to be met at a fixed time

The method of operating is simply an example of what we have so fully illustrated in the preceding chapters, that the *Release of a Debt* is in all cases equivalent to a Payment in Money : or that $- \times - = + \times +$

Instead of transmitting vast amounts of Coin, the method always adopted in such cases is to purchase Bills of Exchange on the place of payment : and by operating on a number of different centres to prevent the disturbances which would arise from withdrawing too large an amount of Circulating Medium from any one place

In 1794 the English Government agreed to lend the Emperor of Germany £4,000,000 : and the problem was to send the money from London to Vienna with as little disturbance as possible to the London money market

Mr. Boyd, who conducted the operation says—" The remittance of so large a sum as £4,000,000 I considered a matter of infinite difficulty and delicacy so as to prevent its producing any remarkable effects on the course of Exchange

" It was necessary to vary the modes of remitting, and to make use of the various means for that purpose presented by all the different Exchanges of Europe.   It was not necessary to remit Bills upon Hamburg only, because it frequently happened that it answered better to remit to Hamburg upon other places, such as Madrid, Cadiz, Leghorn, Lisbon, Genoa, &c., than to remit direct on Hamburg : and having constantly orders from Vienna with regard to the rates of the different remittances to be made, our attention was directed to the accomplishment of these orders on the best possible terms.   In fine, it was necessary to take Bullion, Bills direct upon Hamburg, and Bills upon other places, all into our means of remittance, without giving the decided preference to that mode which was the most favorable, because any one mode invariably adhered to would soon have exhausted and destroyed that mode : whereas by turning occasionally to all the modes, and not sticking too long to any one particular mode, we had the good fortune to make, upon the whole, very favorable remittances "

McCulloch gives another example of a similar operation :—
"In 1804, Spain was bound to pay to France a large subsidy, and
in order to do this, three distinct methods presented themselves.
First, to send dollars to Paris by land : second, to remit Bills of
Exchange direct on Paris : thirdly, to authorise Paris to draw
directly on Spain. The first of these methods was tried, but
found too slow and expensive : and the second and third plans
were considered likely to turn the Exchange against Spain. The
following method, by the indirect or circular Exchange, was
therefore adopted :—

"A merchant or *banquier* at Paris was appointed to manage
the operation, which was thus conducted. He chose London,
Amsterdam, Hamburg, Cadiz, Madrid, and Paris as the principal
hinges upon which the operation was to turn : and he engaged
correspondents in each of these cities to support the circulation.
Madrid and Cadiz were the places in Spain from whence remittances were to be made : and dollars were, of course, to be sent
when they bore the highest price : for which Bills were to be
procured on Paris, or any other place that might be deemed more
advantageous. The principle being thus established, it only
remained to regulate the extent of the operation, so as not to
issue too much paper on Spain, and to give the circulation as
much support as possible from real business. With this view
London was chosen as a place to which the operation might
be chiefly directed, as the price of dollars was then high in
England, a circumstance which rendered the proportional exchange advantageous to Spain

" The business commenced at Paris, where the negotiation of
drafts issued on Hamburg and Amsterdam served to answer the
immediate demands of the state : and orders were transmitted to
these places, to draw for the reimbursement on London, Madrid,
or Cadiz, according as the course of exchange was most favorable.
The proceedings were all conducted with judgement, and attended
with complete success "

But the most gigantic operation of this nature which ever
took place, was the payment of the indemnity France had to pay
to Germany, in consequence of the unfortunate result to her of
the war. A minute account of this operation was presented to

the National Assembly by M. Léon Say, from which we take the following details, sufficient, we hope, to make a general outline of the operation intelligible

By the definitive treaty of peace between Germany and France, signed at Frankfort, May 10, 1871, France became bound to pay the sum of 5 milliards of francs, equal to about 200 millions sterling, at the following dates—500 millions thirty days after the restoration of order in Paris : 1,000 millions in the course of 1871 : 500 millions on May 1, 1872 : and 3,000 millions on March 2, 1874 : together with 5·per cent. interest on the last three milliards

Payment might be made in gold or silver, Notes of the Banks of England, Prussia, Holland, Belgium, or first-class Bills of Exchange

The thaler was valued at 3·75 francs, and the German florin at 2·15 francs

All Bills not domiciled (*i.e.*, made payable) in Germany, were to be valued at their net proceeds, after deducting all costs of collection

The portion of the Eastern Railway of France, situated in Alsace, was accepted as part payment of the Debt to the amount of 325 millions : also 125 millions were received in Notes of the Bank of France : and the sum of 98,400 francs, which remained due to the city of Paris, after the payment of the indemnity exacted from her, were counted as payment on account of the debt of France

Besides the indemnity payable by France, the city of Paris had to pay an indemnity of 200 millions of francs : 50 millions in specie : 50 millions in Notes of the Bank of France : $37\frac{1}{2}$ millions in two months' Bills on Berlin, at the exchange of 3·75 francs for the thaler : and 63 millions in Bills upon London, at six and fifteen days' sight, at 25·20 francs for the pound sterling

The Bills upon London were bought at the exchange of 25·3488 : and those on Berlin at the exchange of 3·7325 : Paris, therefore, lost 44·88 cents. on each pound sterling : and gained 1·75 cent. on each thaler. The total cost of the indemnity was 1,965,240·30 francs : and after it was all settled, there remained a balance of 98,400 francs in favor of Paris, which was carried to the account of the indemnity due from France

The total operation was divided into two parts: the payment of the first two milliards, and that of the last three

In order to put the Government in funds to effect the payment they negotiated a loan of 1,530 millions with the Bank of France: and created two public debts of 2,225,994,045 and of 3,498,744,639 francs

The Government being thus in funds commenced its exchange operations, and the Debt was finally liquidated in the following way—

By Compensations	325,098,400 francs
By Bank Notes and German Money..	742,334,079 francs
By Bills of Exchange	4,248,326,374·26 francs

To effect this stupendous operation all the great bankers in Europe were invited to assist: and in June, 1871, a London agency was opened to assist, and receive subscriptions and bills. Other agencies were opened at Brussels, Amsterdam, Berlin, Frankfort, and Hamburg. In the first loan the pound sterling was received at 25·30: the thaler at 3·75: the Frankfort florin at 7 florins for 4 thalers: the marc banco at 2 marcs for one thaler: and Belgian paper at par. In the second loan the pound sterling was received at 25·43: the thaler at 3·76: the Frankfort florin at 2·14⅞: the marc banco at 1·87⅞ for 1 thaler: and Belgian paper at par

The exchange operations in London began in June, 1871, and lasted till September, 1873. The mean average of the whole was 25·4943

In the course of the operation, the Treasury purchased 120,000 foreign bills, amounting to about 4½ milliards. It opened subscriptions in foreign countries, and received foreign bills in payment of the loan opened in Paris. The subscriptions to the first loan comprised 213 millions, and the subscription to the second loan 389 millions in foreign bills

M. Léon Say then gives some details respecting the three classes above named as Compensations: Bank Notes and German money: and Bills of Exchange

These compensations included—

Notes of the Bank of France	.. ..	125,000,000 francs
German Notes and Money ..	.. ..	105,039,145 francs
French Gold Money	.. ..	273,003,058 francs
French Silver Money	.. ..	239,291,875 francs

The German Bank Notes and Money were collected from the sums which the German armies had brought with them in the invasion

The third class, viz., Bills of Exchange, included German bills taken at their full value, 2,799,514,183·72 francs : and other foreign bills taken at their net proceeds, after deducting all charges, 1,448,812,190·54

M. Léon Say then gives some details of the commercial operations undertaken to support these gigantic payments, but he at once acknowledges that it is impossible to explain their complete theory, on account of a new article of merchandise, which has only recently been introduced into commerce

" It is not possible to explain the operations of a portfolio which contains 120,000 bills of a value exceeding 4 milliards

" There were all sorts of bills, from less than a thousand francs to more than five millions: some mentioned the purchase of merchandise : others appeared to be only fabricated for the purpose, and destined themselves to be covered at maturity by bills which were to be created to pay real transactions

" Bank credits, the paper circulating between head offices and branches, circular exchanges, payments for invoices, the remission of funds for the ultimate purchase of merchandise, the settlement of debts abroad to France under the forms of coupons, shares, and commercial obligations, were all in these effects, making up the most gigantic portfolio which was ever brought together

" After all this, to give a detailed classification is an absolutely impossible task. One can do no more than determine the classes of the operation, and make some general remarks on these classes, and on the importance and meaning of the business effected on each of them

" Fifty years ago there were no other international operations than merchandise and money : merchandise, gold and silver were the only subjects of export and import : the balance of commerce was settled in gold and silver. Everything which was bought from the foreigner was paid for in gold and silver, if not in merchandise.

" One might find, then, in the custom house *data* more or less exact, but at least real *data*, of the course of business between two countries : but things have greatly changed within fifty years

"There has appeared, especially within the last 25 years, in international commerce, what may be called *a new article of export*, an article which in every country has acquired a greater importance than any other, and which has had the result of completely distorting the meaning of Custom House returns. *This new article is* **Securities** : it is transmitting across the frontiers of different states the property of capital by representation, which is easy to transport, viz., these Capitals of the form of Bills of Exchange, Public Funds, Shares and Obligations of Railways, and other Companies

" To understand the real course of international business, it is necessary to know not only the imports and exports of merchandise, the imports and exports of specie, but also the *imports and exports of* **Securities** : and this last class, which is the most important, and which is the key to the two others : escapes all kinds of returns "

This is exactly the doctrine we have been enforcing for so many years : and shows the profound error of those economists who would exclude Incorporeal Property from the title of wealth : and of those who write books on economics, and who are either ignorant of, or ignore its existence : for in this great mercantile country it is now the largest kind of Property of any : and forms an enormous article of export and import between countries

Of the whole French indemnity 273 millions were paid in French gold coin : and 239 millions in French silver coin : being somewhat over 20 millions sterling : whereas 4¼ milliards, or 160 millions sterling, were paid by bills of exchange. Thus little more than one-tenth part of the indemnity was paid in actual specie

In recent years it has been the custom for foreign Governments to raise loans in the English market.   So also foreign companies seek to raise capital in England.   All these loans act upon the Exchanges.   There are also the drafts of families who reside abroad : these drafts act upon the Exchanges exactly in the same manner as any other drafts

On the India Council Bills

32.   Very extensive Exchange operations take place on account of the Government of India

India has to make very large and continuous payments in London on several accounts, such as the interest on the public debt payable in London : the military and civil pension list : the military charges for the transport of British troops to India, and military stores : civil stores of all sorts : and the establishment of the India Office, and the Engineering College at Cooper's Hill

To meet these charges the Council of India in London draws every Wednesday a certain amount of Bills on the Governments of the different Presidencies

In 1880-81 the sum total of disbursements to be made in London exceeded 18 millions sterling : which were all payable in fixed amounts in Gold

But ,the Indian Governments pay in Silver Rupees : it is therefore requisite to draw for such a sum in Rupees as shall produce the required amount in Gold in London

It is for this reason that the relative Value of Gold and Silver is of such deep importance to the Government of India.   Every penny which the rupee falls in value, costs India £1,000,000 sterling

The great importance of these Bills, however, is the effect they have on the Market Price of Silver : they have, in fact, in recent years been a very potent factor in causing the diminished value of Silver with respect to Gold

Selling Bills for Silver in the London market is in reality exactly the same thing as selling so much silver itself.   Consequently, the more these Bills are pressed for sale, the more it must diminish the value of Silver

The Government Rupee, which since 1862 has replaced the old Company's rupee of the same weight and fineness, is 180 grains : being 165 grains fine with 15 of alloy

The British Shilling, coined at the rate of 66 to the lb. weight of Silver Buillion, contains $80\frac{8}{11}$ grains of fine silver : and the florin contains $161\frac{4}{11}$ grains of fine silver

When the price of British standard silver is 60d. per ounce, the rupee is worth 1s. 10·2973d. or nearly 1s. 10·3d. sterling

But ever since 1872-73 there has been a continuous fall in the value of silver : so that at the present time it is only worth $42\frac{5}{8}d.$: or the rupee is only worth 1s. $4\frac{5}{16}d.$

In recent years several causes have combined greatly to reduce the value of silver : these are the increased production of the metal : the demonetisation of silver by Germany : the break up of the Latin Union : and the greatly increased amount of the India Council Bills : these last increased from 8 millions in 1870-71 to 15 millions in 1880-81, having all the effect of an increase of silver to an equal amount

On Monetary and Political Convulsions as affecting the Exchanges

33. As an immediate consequence of the preceding principles, it follows that a Monetary or Political convulsion in a country will immediately turn the Exchanges in favor of that country : if such an event is not prevented by the issue of inconvertible Paper Money. The reason is plain : any political or monetary convulsion is attended by a great destruction of **Credit**. That Credit, while it existed, performed the functions of Money : but as soon as it is destroyed, there is an intense demand for Money to fill the void. Money rises enormously in value. Multitudes of persons are obliged to sell their goods at a sacrifice. The consequence is that Money having risen greatly in value, both with respect to Goods and Debts, flows in from neighbouring countries

In 1800 there was a great commercial crisis at Hamburg. The rate of discount rose to 15 per cent. That immediately drained the Bullion from the Bank of England. In 1825 there was a great commercial crisis in England. For a considerable period the Bank, by making extravagant issues at a low rate of discount, had turned the Exchanges against the country. But, no sooner did the crisis occur in December than the Exchanges immediately became favorable. Exactly the same thing happened in 1847. No sooner had the crisis fairly set in than the Exchanges turned in favor of the country

In the French Revolution in 1793 and subsequent years, the Government issued immense quantities of inconvertible Paper Money, which depressed the Exchanges almost to nothing : in fact at one time they ceased to be quoted. But in 1796 these Assignats were abolished : and the Exchanges immediately turned in favor of France

This has been observed so universally, and the reasons for it are so obvious, that it is needless to quote any more instances

On the **Means** *of* **Correcting** *an* **Adverse Exchange**

34. It has now been shown upon what complicated causes the great movements of Bullion depend, which produce such important consequences. There are Three great Economic Quantities—**Products, Bullion, and Debts**—all seeking to be exchanged, all flowing from where they are cheaper to where they are dearer

But all this vast superstructure of **Credit**—this mighty mass of Merchandise, or exchangeable property—is based upon **Bullion.** Different methods of doing business require different quantities of Bullion: but however highly organised, perfect, and refined, the system may be, we come, at last, to the basis of Bullion as its moderator and regulator. If, therefore, the Bullion be suffered to ebb away too rapidly, the whole superstructure is endangered, and then ensues one of those dreadful calamities—a Monetary Crisis

We have endeavoured to explain the different causes which produce an adverse exchange: so that if one takes place the proper corrective may be applied. If it be caused by a Depreciated Currency, there is no cure but a restoration of the Currency to its proper state

When, however, it arises from a balance of indebtedness from commercial transactions, there are but two methods of correcting it—an **Export of Produce,** *or a* **Rise in the Rate of Discount.**

It used to be a favorite doctrine that an adverse exchange was, in itself, an inducement to export produce on account of the premium at which the Bills could be sold. What truth there was in this doctrine can only be known to those actually engaged in such operations.   But a very much more certain means of producing an export of goods is a **Lowering of their Price**

This was one of the fundamental objects of the framers of the Bank Charter Act of 1844. They truly observed that the prices of goods had often been unduly inflated by the excessive creation of Credit, while gold was rapidly flowing out of the country.   Thus, when the prices of goods were kept too high here, they, of course, could not be exported to countries where they were cheaper: and, consequently, nothing but gold would go. One object of the Act, therefore, was by causing a gradual and compulsory contraction of Credit as Bullion ebbed away, to lower the price of goods and encourage an export of them

The reasoning of the framers of the Act was undoubtedly correct in that respect. But the only question is, whether they hit upon the right method of producing the effect they desired: and whether the same object may not be attained by another and a better method.   This, however, is not the place to discuss fully the policy of that Act: because there are several other conflicting theories involved in it: which we cannot fully discuss until we come to explain the mechanism of the Act itself, and its operation during a commercial crisis

It is sufficient to state here that all the objects of that Act are attained by paying proper attention to raise the Rate of Discount as rapidly as Bullion flows out. If the Directors of the Bank had understood and acted upon that principle, although there would necessarily, in the nature of things, have been Commercial Crises, there would never have been Monetary Panics, or any necessity for that Act. It was to not understanding and acting upon this principle that all the Monetary troubles of the last three-quarters of a century have been due. It is true that we cannot blame them too much, as before 1833 interest by law was restricted to 5 per cent., a rate wholly inadequate to check a great outflow of Bullion : and for many years it was held to be a theological sin to charge more than 5 per cent.

It has been shown that a difference in the Rate of Discount between two places exceeding the cost of sending Bullion from one to the other, causes a flow of Bullion from one to the other. But as all the cost of sending bullion both ways falls upon the operator, the difference will be greater than might appear at first sight.   And if the Bills be three months, the profit realised will only be one-fourth of the apparent difference.   Mr. Goschen says that there must be a difference of 2 per cent. between London and Paris before the operation of sending over gold to or from France for the sake of the interest will pay.   And between other continential cities, of course, the difference may be much greater

But whatsoever the difference may be, the **Method** is absolutely certain.   Directly the Rate of Discount is raised here, persons cease to export Bullion from this country : and the continental bankers and brokers increase their demand for English Bills. And as the Rate rises the demand will increase, until the price reaches the Specie point, and gold flows in : and as the Rate rises more, more powerful will be the attraction, until at last the necessary equilibrium is restored between **Bullion** and **Credit**

CHAPTER IX

ON THE NATURE OF THE FUNDS

1. The nature of the Funds has always been an inscrutable enigma to those persons who adhere to the exploded concept of Economics as the " Production, Distribution and Consumption of Wealth "

If a person had £500,000, as it is termed, in the Funds, he would be acknowledged to be a "wealthy" person.   But when the Funds themselves are said to be Wealth, many persons are scandalised at the idea that Public Debts are Public Wealth

It is obvious that the Public Debts, or Public Credit, depends upon exactly the same principles as the Credit of private persons, of which we have elaborately explained the principles and the mechanism in the preceding chapters

Before, however, we proceed to the exposition of the subject, it will be expedient to clear away the errors with which it is infested

Error of Mill and others regarding the Nature of the Funds

2.   It is first of all necessary to point out a most serious error which many persons hold regarding the nature of the Funds

Thus, Mill says[1]—" This leads to an important distinction in the meaning of the word Wealth as applied to the possessions of the individual, and to those of a nation or of mankind.   In the Wealth of mankind, nothing is included which does not of itself answer some purpose of use or pleasure (?).   To an individual anything is Wealth which, though useless in itself, enables him to claim from others a part of their stock of things useful or pleasant.

[1]*Preliminary Remarks*

"Take, for instance, a mortgage of one thousand pounds on a landed estate. This is Wealth to the person to whom it brings a revenue, and who could perhaps sell it in the market for the full amount of the debt. But it is not Wealth to the country; if the engagement were annulled the country would be neither poorer nor richer. The mortgagee would have lost a thousand pounds, and the owner of the land would have gained it. Speaking nationally the mortgage was not itself Wealth but merely gave A a claim to a portion of the wealth of B. It was wealth to A, and wealth which he could transfer to a third person : but what he so transferred was, in fact, a joint ownership, to the extent of a thousand pounds in the land of which B was nominally the sole proprietor

"The position of the fundholders, or owners of the public debt of the country, is similar. *They are mortgagees on the general Wealth of the country.* The cancelling of the debt would be no *destruction* of wealth, but a *transfer* of it: a wrongful abstraction of wealth from certain members of the community for the benefit of the Government, or of the taxpayers. *Funded property, therefore, cannot be counted as part of the national wealth.* This is not always borne in mind by the dealers in statistical calculations. For example, in estimates of the gross incomes of the country, founded on the proceeds of the Income Tax, incomes derived from the Funds are not always excluded : though the taxpayers are assessed on their whole nominal income, without being permitted to deduct from it the portion levied from them in taxation to form the income of the fundholder. In the calculation, therefore, one portion of the general income of the country is counted twice over, and the aggregate amount made to appear greater than it is by almost thirty millions. A country, however, may include in its wealth all stock held by its citizens in the funds of foreign countries, and other debts due to them from abroad. But even this is only wealth to them by being a part ownership in wealth held by others. It forms no part of the collective wealth of the human race. It is an element in the distribution, but not in the composition, of the general wealth "

The fallacy that the Funds are similar to a mortgage, appears conspicuously in another writer, Mr. Capps, who gained a prize of £200 put at the disposal of the Society of Arts, for the best essay on the mode of liquidating the National Debt

He says—" There are two antagonistic and conflicting fallacies respecting the National Debt which are very prevalent. The first is that funded property forms as much a portion of the wealth of the country, and is, therefore, to be reckoned among its assets, as lands, houses, or any other description of tangible property. The second which is precisely the opposite of the former is that the Debt is a subtraction or a deduction from the wealth of the country: that the country is so much the poorer for it. Neither the one nor the other is correct: for the truth is that the country, with the trifling exception which we shall hereafter name, is neither the richer nor the poorer for the existence of the debt, and that, consequently, both the opinions we have mentioned as being prevalent are erroneous: which we shall now proceed to show

" With regard to the first, we have seen estimates made of the total wealth of the country in which, after the enumeration as a portion of the wealth of the nation of lands, houses, raw materials, and manufactured products of all descriptions, there has been an item inserted of ' Funded Property,' which has been considered as of itself an actual property, separate from, and an addition to, all other wealth. Now the debt or the funds, though a property to the parties who hold them, are not so to the nation as a whole: for they are only *a Mortgage upon the rest of the Property of the country:* and by just so much as they are the property of the holders, they are an incumbrance and a diminution of the value of the things so mortgaged or incumbered

" It is precisely a parallel case to the following :—A is worth £10,000 in the shape of an estate of that value. B is worth £5,000 in money. A mortgages his estate to B for £5,000, and spends the money unproductively. Let now a valuation be made of the property of A and B jointly, and we shall find that the amount of their united wealth is just the value of the estate, and nothing more. The estate is worth £10,000, £5,000 of which belongs to B as mortgagee, and £5,000 the value of the equity of redemption to A as mortgagor. The mortgage in no way adds to the value of the estate : and though it is a property to B as mortgagee, it is to the same extent a diminution to A of the value of the estate "

The glaring absurdity of this statement is obvious. Before the transaction Mr. Capps admits the united property of A and B to be £10,000 + £5,000, or £15,000 : and then after the transaction the united value of their property is £10,000 : so that by some marvelous hocus pocus, £5,000 of value has disappeared !

Mr. Capps then proceeds—" It is the same with the national Debt. The whole country and its productions are mortgaged to the fundholder to the extent of about one-seventh of their value : and though such funds form a property to the holders of them, they are only so in the character of a mortgage which reduces the value of the property mortgaged to its proprietor by just the amount of the mortgage. In taking, therefore, any account, or making any valuation of the total wealth of the country, funded property must not be put down as an item unless you make a corresponding deduction, on the other hand, from the value of the property of which it forms a mortgage "

We have quoted these passages at somewhat wearisome length, in order that we may not be supposed to have misrepresented the writers. They contain a complete series of misconceptions and errors upon a subject of great importance, and which involve several of the fundamental concepts of Economics

Error of considering the **Funds** as a **Mortgage** on the **Property** of the Country

3. To consider the Funds as a Mortgage on the lands and property of the country is a gross and palpable error which only arises from ignorance of the most elementary principles of Mercantile Law

A Mortgage is a formal deed conveying rights to certain property. Now when were the fundholders ever put by a formal deed of conveyance into possession of the country and its productions ? Let us see the Act of Parliament which did so. Until the deed of conveyance which gave over the country and its productions to the fundholders can be produced, it is clear that the Funds are not similar to a mortgage on the property of the country

As a matter of pure Jurisprudence, the Funds and a Mortgage deed belong to two totally different classes of property

In English law when a person borrows money on mortgage, as it is termed, he actually sells the land to the mortgagee in exchange for the money ; and a mortgage deed is the title to that specific land and to no other. The mortgage becomes the actual legal owner of the land : but he is bound to re-sell or re-convey the land to the mortgagor upon his repaying the money. Hence a Mortgage deed is not separate property from the land : it forms but one property with it. Just as Bills of Lading and Dock Warrants are titles to specific goods. Such documents are *not* Credit : they are **Jura in re**

The Funds are not a mortgage on the **Property** of the country : they are a charge on the **Income** of the country : they are a Bill of Exchange payable by instalments for ever

When a merchant gives a Bill of Exchange in exchange for goods, it is not a right to any Specific money : it is a charge only against his person : he merely engages that he shall be in possession of some money when the bill falls due to pay it : and therefore it is called a **Credit**

So when the State borrows money and gives the Right, called the Funds in exchange, they are not the Right to any specific lands or products, but are a mere charge against the State as a *persona* in its corporate capacity : and they are intended to be paid out of its future income. They are therefore called **Public Credit**

To suppose that the Funds are a mortgage on the land and its productions is as gross an error as to suppose that when a merchant accepts a Bill of Exchange it is a Mortgage on his lands and house

The Funds, like Bills of Exchange, are **Credit**: they both belong to the class of property termed **Jura in personam**

Mill is also grossly in error when he says the citizens of one country may include in their wealth the stocks held by them of foreign countries, and other debts due to them from abroad : but that it forms no part of the collective wealth of the human race, because it is only wealth to them as part ownership in wealth held by others.

This involves the very common, but gross, error that a Creditor has a Right in the property of his debtor. But every jurist in the world has pointed out, as we have fully shown already, that a Creditor has no right in the property of his debtor. A debtor's property is absolutely his own : and all that the Creditor has, is a Right of action against his person to compel him to exchange some of his property to buy up the Right of action against himself. The Right of action and the Debtor's property, therefore, are two separate and distinct articles of property : and there is no joint ownership whatever

Are the Incomes of the Fundholders to be reckoned separately in the General Income of the Country?

4. Mill then alleges that it is a statistical error to count the incomes of the fundholders as independent incomes in the income of the country, as they are already paid by the taxpayers, and that to count them as separate incomes is to count the same sum twice over.

Now if this doctrine is true—if it is a theoretical error of statisticians to count the incomes of the fundholders as separate incomes in the general income of the country, it is equally a practical error in the Chancellor of the Exchequer to charge the fundholders with Income Tax : for it is very evident that he considers them as separate taxable incomes

Considering the reputation that Mill formerly enjoyed as an Economist, though it is now utterly exploded among all intelligent persons, it is somewhat surprising that this doctrine, which is so comfortable for the fundholders, seems never to have attracted their attention. If it is true, why do not the fundholders in a body memorialise the Chancellor of the Exchequer to exempt them from the Income Tax, on the plan that their incomes have already been taxed in the general income of the country ? For if it is a statistical error to count the same sum twice over in the general income of the country, it is equally a practical error to tax the same sum twice over

And if an obdurate Chancellor of the Exchequer turns a deaf ear to their memorial, why should they not take measures to have the question tried in a Court of Law ?

The doctrine no doubt is somewhat specious, and requires investigation : but we shall find that in this case, as in so many others, Mill asserts a doctrine which hits a great many other cases besides the one he has in veiw

If the argument is true that the incomes of the fundholders must be excluded from the general income because they are already paid by the taxpayers, it applies to a great many other cases : because many other incomes are paid out of the taxes of the country

1. The Crown : the civil list of the Crown is paid out of the taxes of the country : therefore it is not a separate income : and therefore it ought not to be taxed

2. The Military and Naval services : the pay of all soldiers and sailors is paid out of the taxes of the country : therefore they are not separate incomes : and therefore they ought not to be taxed

3. The Civil service : the whole of the Civil service from the Prime Minister and the Lord Chancellor down to the humblest policeman are paid out of the taxes and rates : therefore their incomes are not separate incomes : and therefore they ought not to be taxed

If Mill's argument is true, the incomes of all these persons must be excluded from the catalogue of the national income, because they all stand on the same footing as the fundholders : they are all paid out of the taxes of the country : and for the same reason they ought not to pay Income Tax

Are believers in Mill prepared to adopt these conclusions ? If his argument is true, how can they escape from them ?

But if Mill's argument is true, it must be applied to many other cases besides those of persons who receive continuous salaries paid out of the taxes of the country for rendering continuous services to the State

Many persons do it a temporary service, and are paid out of the taxes of the country. If Mill's argument is true, the sums paid by the state for these services are not a separate income because they are paid out of the taxes : and they ought not to be taxed

The Government frequently contracts with private firms to do work for the State : with ship builders to build ironclads : or guns : with contractors to supply clothing, arms, beef, pork, rum, and other stores of all sorts : also with private firms for building the public offices

All these contractors are paid out of the taxes of the country.

If Mill's argument is true, the sums paid to these contractors ought not to be counted in their incomes : and they ought not to be taxed

Are believers in Mill prepared to adopt these conclusions ? If his argument is true, how can they escape from them ?

But if Mill's argument is true it must be still further greatly extended : for many persons derive their incomes from those of other persons : and yet they both pay Income Tax

A great nobleman has an income of perhaps £100,000 a year, he keeps a French cook, perhaps at £300 a year : and a Scotch gardener at £250 a year : and a retinue of other domestics

Now it is evident that the incomes of all his employés and domestics come out of my lord's income : and yet they are each reckoned separately in the income of the country : and my lord pays Income Tax on his income : and each of his employés whose salary is above the limit, pays Income Tax on his income

In short, if Mill's argument is true, the salary of no person whatever, who is in the service of any other person whatever, single or corporate, ought to be counted as a separate income, and he ought not to be taxed for it

Are believers in Mill prepared to adopt these conclusions ? If his argument is true how can they escape from them ?

But to bring the matter to a conclusion it is easy to show that the income of every trade, business, and profession whatever is paid in succession out of the general income of the country

Every person's Income is paid out of the Income of someone else

The doctrine stated thus abruptly may seem like a paradox. Nevertheless a very slight explanation, with the assistance of the acknowledged fundamental truths of modern Economics, will very soon unravel the paradox. And it is contained in the observation of Smith that the same pieces of money pay everyone's income in succession

It has been shown that one of the great advances in Economics made by Smith and Condillac was that in an exchange *both* sides gain

The proposition that we have stated, that every person's income comes out of the income of some one else, is the necessary consequence of Smith's observation, that the same pieces of money pay everyone's income in succession, and that in an exchange both sides gain

Let us take a few examples

It is obviously true of all professional men. Where do the incomes of lawyers and medical men come from ? Evidently from the incomes of their clients and patients. Where do the incomes of actors and musical performers come from ? Evidently from the incomes of their audiences. And the incomes of all these persons are justly reckoned separately in the general income of the country.

Owners of land devote their labor and capital to produce corn and cattle, because they know that the public want to be clothed and fed. And they make an income by so doing. And where does their income come from ? Evidently from the incomes of the persons who want to be clothed and fed

Merchants bestow their labor and capital in importing foreign commodities into the country : and by so doing they make an income. And where does their income come from ? Evidently from the incomes of the persons who want their commodities

Landowners having earned an income by selling corn and cattle, expend their income on their employés, or butchers, bakers, tailors, lawyers, doctors, and public amusements

Merchants having earned an income by importing or exporting commodities, as the case may be, expend that income on their clerks and servants, educating their children. upon butchers, bakers, tailors, and places of public amusement

Lawyers. doctors, engineers, actors, having earned an income from their clients and patients, expend that income upon educating their children, upon butchers, bakers, tailors and public amusements.

And this mechanism is true of all occupations and trades in succession. In fact the whole mechanism of society is a series of exchanges : and in all exchanges there is profit

Each party in the exchange earns an income, and he pays an income on that

Contractors earn an income from private persons by doing them services : by building houses, ships, &c.; and they pay Income Tax on their profits. They do the State services by building ships, guns, public offices, and in innumerable other ways ; and they earn an income by so doing, just in the same way as by doing a similar service to a private person : and therefore they pay Income Tax on their profits ; equally in one case as the other

So also the Professions and the Civil Service, Ministers, Judges, Naval and Military men do the State a service, and earn an income by so doing. And the income they earn is a separate income, just as much as if they had done the service to a private person. And therefore they pay Income Tax equally in one case as the other

If Mill's doctrine were true, a lawyer who earns an income by fees from private clients should pay Income Tax; but a Judge who earns an income by doing a service to the State, and receives a salary for so doing, out of the taxes should pay no Income Tax

But no Chancellor of the Exchequer or Court of Law would listen to such an argument for a moment

Mill's argument, therefore, is entirely erroneous as applied to the fundholders, and all the preceding cases

The case where it does apply is where a father makes his son an allowance to keep him at college : in this case the youth does nothing to earn an income : it is a pure gratuity : it comes out of his father's income, who receives no service in exchange for it : such an allowance is no more to be reckoned as part of the income of the country than the sum spent by a father in maintaining his children at home is part of the income of the country

Suppose, again, a father has a son in the Guards, and finding his pay not sufficient to enable him to maintain him suitably to his position in society, makes him an allowance. Then the pay he receives is part of the income of the country, because it is earned in exchange for a service done : the allowance he receives from his father is not income : it is mere expenditure on the part of the father. Accordingly, the officer pays Income Tax on his pay : but not on the allowance he receives from his father

So when a person makes an allowance to his poor relations, they pay no Income Tax on the amount so received in charity

But the fundholders receive an income in exchange for a service done to the State : and accordingly their income is part of the general income of the country, just as if they had lent their money to a private person : and accordingly they pay Income Tax upon it

Mill's reason for saying that the Funds are not part of the National Wealth

6. Mill says—"The canceling of the debt would be no *destruction* of wealth, but a *transfer* of it, a wrongful transfer of it from certain members of the community for the profit of the Government, or of the taxpayers. Funded property, therefore, cannot be counted as part of National wealth"

This seems a most extraordinary conclusion. A *transfer* of wealth is, in no case that we can imagine, the destruction of it. But Mill says that because the *transfer* of it is not the *destruction* of it, therefore it is not to be counted as part of the national wealth

A highwayman knocks down a traveller and robs him of his watch and money : now this is only a *transfer* of the watch and money : it is not a *destruction* of them : *therefore*, according to Mill, the watch and the money form no part of the national wealth !

A servant robs his master : that is only a *transfer* and not a *destruction* of the thing stolen : *therefore* the thing stolen forms no part of the national wealth !

We wonder what kind of syllogism leads to such a conclusion ?

There is no doubt a considerable degree of subtlety about the question, but most assuredly Mill's reason throws no light upon it

On the true Nature of the Funds

7. Having now cleared away all these errors and misconceptions as to the nature of the Funds, we shall now explain their real nature

It has been shown in a former chapter that the State in its corporate capacity is a **Persona,** quite independent of its individual citizens. That it can buy and sell and exchange in that capacity exactly like a private individual : and that with its own citizens as well as with any one else : just as a public company can deal with its own shareholders

It has also been shown that an annuity is an economic quantity quite separate and independent of the sums of money actually paid : and that it can be bought and sold quite separately from them

It has also been shown that every sum of money is equivalent to an annuity, either perpetual or limited : consequently, that an annuity may be sold for money : *i.e.*, that they are each exchangeable quantities : and may be exchanged like any material chattels

Moreover, the State has an income like any private person

This being so, the State in its corporate capacity has **Purchasing Power,** like any private individual : and it may buy a sum of money by giving in exchange for it an annuity : or the Right to receive a series of payments, either perpetual or for a limited time : to be paid out of its future income

That is to say, the Credit of the State, just like the Credit of a private individual, brings into Commerce the Present Value or the Present Right to its future income

Now the State in its corporate capacity has to perform certain duties, and is often in want of a considerable sum of money for some emergency, as a war : or to provide for a public famine : or to create some great public work, such as a Railroad or a Canal

In order to effect these purposes it buys a present sum of money and gives in exchange for it an annuity : or the Right to receive a series of payments out of its future income. The money becomes the absolute property of the State, and the annuities become the property of the subscribers to the Loan

In legal language this Annuity is termed a **Bank Annuity**: because, as we have shown, the original meaning of the word **Banco**, or Bank, is a Public Debt. In former times it was also called a **Rent**: but this name has quite gone out of use in England : though it is still the usual name for the Funds on the Continent

In granting these Perpetual Annuities the State never binds itself to pay off the principal : hence in popular language they are called the **Funds**: because the capital sum is *founded*, or *fixed*. The State, however, reserves to itself the right to pay off the annuities if it pleases to do so. If the fundholder wants to get back his capital he can sell his Annuity to any one else. The Funds are therefore marketable or vendible commodities, just like any material chattels

The Funds are therefore Property of exactly the same nature as the shares in a public company. The individual shareholders pay over their money to the Company as a **Persona,** and receive in exchange for it the Right to share in the future profits of the Company. The Funds are therefore simply a mass of Exchangeable Property, similar to Bills of Exchange, Annuities, and all other Incorporeal Property

They are all simply the present Rights to future payments

On the **Ratio** *of the* **Public Debt** *to the* **Wealth** *of the Country*

8. We shall now observe the evil consequences in Economics of the want of clear fundamental concepts

Mr. Capps values the **Wealth** of the country at £6,000,000,000, and he says that the National Debt is about one-seventh of the **Wealth** of the country

But what does Mr. Capps mean by the **Wealth** of the country ?

Even taking the Wealth of the country as its *material* property only, such an estimate is manifestly utterly inadequate. Taking a very moderate estimate of the value of the land upon which London is built, it will be found that it exceeds £4,000,000,000 :

and when to this is added the value of the land upon which other great cities, such as Birmingham, Manchester, Liverpool, Leeds, Glasgow, Edinburgh, Bristol, and hosts of others, are built, it will be found that the value of these lands alone exceeds many times the value of the whole wealth of the country

Besides the author of the Eryxias, Smith, and every Economist of note since, have all classed the natural and acquired abilities of all the members of the Society as part of the **Wealth** of the country. Are all these included in Mr. Capps's estimate of the **Wealth** of the country ?

. Moreover, Demosthenes, Adam Smith, and every Economist of note since, all class the Personal Credit of all the merchants, bankers, traders, corporations of all kinds, and the Credit of the State itself as National Wealth. Is all this included in Mr. Capps's estimate of the **Wealth** of the country ?

In addition to these there is that gigantic mass of Property termed Incorporeal Property, including Mercantile and Banking Credits of all kinds : Shares in Commercial Companies of all kinds : the goodwill of all the places of business in the country : practices : copyrights : patents : and many other kinds of valuable Rights. Has **Mr.** Capps included the value of all this kind of property in his estimate of the wealth of the country ?

It is manifest that all estimates of the " **Wealth** " of the country are mere delusions and snares : and of no service for any scientific purposes. It is probable that the real **Wealth** of the country, in its widest estimate, would exceed Mr. Capps's estimate one hundredfold

As a matter of fact, the Funds are not a mortgage on the material products and property of the country : they are a charge upon the **Income** of the nation. The interest of the Debt is not a charge upon those persons only who have an income from material property : but also a charge upon those persons whose incomes are derived from industry of all kinds. The industry of all the professions and of all the intellectual capital is just as much pledged for the payment of the dividends as the incomes of those who have real estate

. The Funds are an Annuity payable out of the income of the entire nation : and consequently their weight upon the public wealth is the Ratio of this Annuity to the General Income of the country

Some persons propose that the Debt should be extinguished by compelling everyone who is possessed of property to give up so much of it. But how are we to compel those persons whose property consists only in their intellectual abilities to give up a part of it? It is possible to confiscate material property. If a man has a thousand acres of land, or ten thousand pounds, the State may take away one hundred acres of his land, or a thousand pounds of his money. But how is the State to confiscate one-tenth of his intellectual capital? A great advocate, physician, engineer, or other professional man makes an income of £10,000 a year. While he does so his talents are as much Capital to him as an estate in land which produces £10,000 a year to its owner. But how is the state to get possession of a tenth part of a professional man's intellectual capital? Is it to take an axe and chop off a bit of his head? It is clear that there is no method of taxing intellectual capital but by taxing its **Profits** or its **Income**. And the industrial income of every advocate, physician, engineer and every artisan is as much pledged for the payment of the funds, as the incomes of men of real estate

It is probable that the ratio of the Funds, so far from being one-seventh of the wealth of the nation is far less than 1 to 100 of its income

Are *the* Funds Wealth?

9. Are, then, the Funds Wealth? This, of course, obviously depends on the meaning of the word **Wealth**? When it is once agreed, as the ancients unanimously held for 1,300 years, and all modern Economists have now come to agree, that the word Wealth simply means any Exchangeable Property—anything whatever which can be bought and sold—whatever its nature or its form may be: it is at once seen that the Funds are Wealth: because they can be bought and sold separately and independently of anything else

So Byles speaks of the Funds as being property only second in magnitude to the land. And Say, in the very commencement of his work, expressly classes the Funds as Wealth?

Mill, indeed, allows that the Funds are wealth to the owners of them ; but, he says, that they are not National Wealth. Now when we say that the word Wealth means nothing but Exchangeable Property, National Wealth can only mean that property which belongs to the nation in its corporate capacity, such as public lands, public forests, dockyards, the navy, &c.: things which do not belong to any private individual. Individual property is certainly not *National* wealth. My money belongs to me and not to the nation

When some persons are horrified at the idea of Debts being termed Wealth they are totally ignorant that the word Debt has two meanings—that it means both the Creditor's **Right of action** as well as the Debtor's **Duty to pay**

Now, no man says that a person's Duty to pay money is part of his Wealth: but every one admits that the Creditor's Right of action is part of his Wealth

The Debtor's Wealth is his **Credit**, or his power of purchasing with his promise to pay at a future time, instead of with actual ready money

Similarly, the Wealth of a State is its Credit, or its power of purchasing sums of money by giving in exchange for them Rights to demand a series of payments in the future times

The case is exactly analogous to a gold mine before the gold is extracted from the mine, and coined, and brought into commerce.

It is usual for popular writers to speak of the mineral wealth of a country : its gold mines, its coal mines, &c.

But, as a technical term in Economics, Economists unanimously held that a thing is not " Wealth " until is is brought into commerce and exchanged

Thus, in Economics, gold mines are not to be held to be " Wealth " until the gold is extracted, coined, and brought into commerce: and extracting gold from the mines coining it, and bringing it into commerce, augments the sum of exchangeable quantities in circulation : and is, therefore, an increase of what, in Economics, is technically termed Wealth

Gold in the mines is in Economics a **Resource**: but it is not " Wealth" until it is brought into commerce

Now, Demosthenes, and all modern Economists, allow that the true definition of Wealth is *anything whatever which has purchasing power*

Now, Personal and State Credit are Purchasing Power: and, therefore, they are Wealth

But Personal and State Credit unused are like gold in the mine. They are a **Resource**

But when persons and the State utilise their Credit by making purchases with them, it is exactly analogous to extracting gold from the mine, coining it, and bringing it into commerce

When private persons and the State utilise their Credit by purchasing with it, they **Coin** their **Credit**: and, just as obtaining gold from the mine, coining it, and bringing it into commerce augments the mass of Exchangeable Quantities: so, when private persons in the State coin their Credit, it augments a mass of Exchangeable Quantities, and this Credit, coined and brought into circulation has, in every respect, identical effects with an equal quantity of gold

But all this Credit, both of private persons and the State, is simply the Present Rights, or the Present Value of future payments

Thus the function of Credit is simply to bring into commerce the Present Values of Future Profits: and that obviously increases the mass of Exchangeable Quantities, or Wealth

We now see the confusion of Mill's distinction between the wealth of mankind and individual wealth. He says that in the wealth of mankind nothing is included which does not of itself answer some purpose of use and pleasure : that to an individual anything is wealth which enables him to claim from others a part of their stock of things

But how can the wealth of mankind be different in its nature from the wealth of individuals ? For the wealth of mankind is made up of the aggregate wealth of individuals

It is evident that in the one case Mill makes wealth depend upon **Utility**: and in the other case upon **Exchangeability**: the very confusion he falls into in his first chapter, and which pervades almost all modern treatises on Economics

But, as the ancients held for 1,300 years, **Exchangeability** is the sole essence and principle of Wealth : and pure Economics is simply the Science which treats of the phenomena relating to Exchangeability

A few examples will show how the utilisation of Credit augments the wealth of a country

When a Company undertakes to construct a public work, a railway, a dock, a canal, or any other, it buys money from its shareholders, and, in exchange for the money, it gives them certificates entitling them to share in the future profits of the company. Thus, the company, as a *Persona*, in its corporate capacity, utilises its credit by buying money from its own Shareholders. It makes the railway, canal, or dock, which produces a permanent revenue : and, according to this revenue, the Shares become a valuable marketable commodity : and are, therefore, Wealth

So, when a Bank is formed it buys money from its shareholders and gives in exchange for it Rights to share in the future profits of the Bank. The Bank then buys money and Bills of Exchange by selling its Credit, or Rights of action, instead of actual money, and some make enormous profits by so doing, and the Shares, or Rights to share in the future profits of the Bank become immensely valuable commodities or wealth

Now, all these gigantic mercantile establishments, producing the revenues of principalities, are just as much Wealth as the land of the country. They are all created by means of Credit

And yet there is not one word about them in the common books on Economics

In some countries and in some of our colonies it is considered as the duty of the State to execute these great public works. But the State has no money at its command to execute them : it must, therefore, utilise its Credit : it contracts public loans to obtain the money : giving in exchange for the money Rights to demand future payments expected to be made out of the future profits of the works : but, at all events, for which the State is liable.

Now these public works being executed by the state and being the property of the State are Public Wealth : and they are executed by the State, utilising its Credit. Hence, we see that these Public Loans have augmented the Public Wealth

Again, suppose that a country is subject to inundations by the sea, and that, to preserve the lives and the property of the inhabitants, it is absolutely necessary to erect vast sea dykes. Now, as these sea dykes are absolutely necessary for the safety of the people, all the inhabitants must contribute to their formation and maintenance

The State, then, being compelled to execute these works without delay, utilises its Credit, and buys large sums of money by giving in exchange for them the Rights to demand future payments out of the taxes of the country

Now, Holland is such a country as we have described. It draws 20 feet of water: and these sea dykes are necessary to preserve its very existence

Now, are the sea dykes part of the "**Wealth**" of Holland? Under the peculiar circumstance of the country they are wanted: they are useful: they are "the product of land and labour:" they cost immense sums of money. Taking the very narrowest view of Wealth that any Economist has taken they answer all the conditions of Wealth

It is clear that they stand in exactly the same position as roads, railways, and canals: and a great quantity of the other Fixed Capital of the country. The people continually want them: and they pay a portion of their annual income to the persons who advanced the money to make them. That forms the income of the persons who lent the money: and it is justly reckoned as a separate item in the catalogue of the general income of the country

But the country may have other wants besides the ones enumerated. It may have enemies by sea and land: and it may be necessary to raise fleets and armies to defend its existence, just as the sea dykes defend the existence of Holland. It may be necessary to contract large public loans for this purpose. The State utilises its Credit by buying large sums of money from private persons, and, giving in exchange for them Rights to demand payments out of the future income of the nation. The persons who sell their money to the State for this purpose do it a service equally as those who sold it their money to erect sea dykes.

M 2

And the Income they receive for performing the service stands exactly on the same footing as the incomes of those who render it any other service whatever

The Funds are, therefore, a mass of Exchangeable Property, exactly of the same nature as Bills of Exchange, Bank Credits, Bank Notes, Shares in Mercantile Companies: the Goodwill of a Business: Copyrights, and all other Incorporeal Property

By contracting Public Loans, the State does exactly as every private person does who utilises his Credit: it brings into Commerce the Present Value of its Future Income

On the method of Contracting Public Debts

10.   Public Debts are contracted in three forms—

(1.)   The Government may be in want of money for current expenses before the taxes come in.   In such a case it gives its own Promissory Notes and sells them in the market: just in the same way as a private person may ask his banker to discount his Note in anticipation of his income.   The banker discounts his Note and retains the profit at the time of the advance.   Private bills are, therefore, always at a discount.   But the Government always wishes its Bills to circulate at par: consequently they always promise such an interest as will keep them at par

These promissory Notes of the Government are termed **Exchequer Bills**: and as they are intended to be paid off at maturity like ordinary Bills of Exchange, they are termed the **Floating** or **Unfunded Debt**

(2)   The Government may want a larger sum than can be met by the usual taxes, and they may buy these larger sums by giving in exchange for them Annuities, terminable at fixed periods.   In such cases the Annuity granted is sufficient to pay not only the interest due on the capital, but a portion of the capital itself: so that, at the termination of that Annuity, the whole principal is paid off, and the Debt extinguished

(3.)   The Government may go into the market, and offer for sale a perpetual annuity of 3, 4, or 5 per cent., and per annum, for what it will fetch.   In this case the Government makes no promise ever to pay off the principal, but they reserve to themselves the right to do so if they please. These perpetual Annuities are what are called, in common parlance, the **Funds**: because the capital is fixed, or founded: and cannot be reclaimed from the State

We have already shown that the original meaning in Italian of **Banco** is a Public Debt: or a sum of money sold to the State by a number of private persons: and called also a **Monte**, or a joint-stock fund. So the legal name of these Public Debts, commonly called the Funds, is **Bank Annuities**

Formerly every new Loan was secured on certain specific branches of public revenue: but this, for many reasons, was found to be inconvenient: so, in the year 1751, all these Debts were consolidated into one sum, and secured on the general revenues of the country. Hence, they were called **Consolidated Bank Annuities**: which, in modern commercial usage, is abbreviated into **Consols**

Sometimes the Floating Debt increases to an inconvenient extent, which cannot be redeemed at once, and the holders of it are induced by the Government to accept an Annuity in place of their right to be paid the capital sum. This is termed **Funding the Unfunded Debt**

It is sometimes said that the Public Debt of Great Britain is about £800,000,000. This, however, is not a correct way of stating it. The country is not bound ever to pay the sum which would constitute it a Debt. What it has contracted to do is to pay an Annuity of about £28,000,000 a year: and the £800,000,000 is simply the Present Value of this perpetual Annuity

CHAPTER X

ON THE INFLUENCE OF MONEY AND CREDIT ON PRICES AND THE RATE OF INTEREST

1. We have now to enter upon an inquiry of the greatest importance and complexity—namely, the influence of Money and Credit on Prices, and the Rate of Interest

In 1873 a great change in the relative Value of Gold and Silver began to take place : and Silver began rapidly to fall in value as compared to Gold.   This produced such inconveniences in the commerce between those countries which used Gold as their standard currency and those which used Silver, that a Royal Commission was appointed to investigate and report on the subject.   With this report, however, we have nothing to do in this place

But Silver continued to fall rapidly in value as compared to Gold, and an unparalleled and continued depression of the prices of products took place throughout the world, and produced such distress that in 1885 a Royal Commission was appointed to investigate its causes

It had been observed that for a few years previously the supplies of gold from the mines had diminished in a slight degree : and it was a very prevalent opinion that the depression in prices, or the appreciation of Gold, as it was termed, was entirely produced by the diminished supplies of Gold

Lord Iddesleigh was chairman of the Commission, and he issued a circular containing a number of questions on the subject. Among other persons to whom Lord Iddesleigh sent this paper was myself.   But upon considering the questions, I found that to give a satisfactory answer to them would require a volume. Moreover, to answer them properly would require a complete exposition of the scientific and juridical principles, and the mechanism of the great system of Credit, of which the general public were profoundly ignorant: and moreover, however distinguished individually the Commissioners were, there was not a single one of them who was a trained mercantile lawyer: so that in order to make the subject intelligible. it would have been necessary to address to the Commission a series of lectures on the Mercantile Law of Credit. Seeing the impossibility of such a course, I thought it advisable not to send in any answers to the paper of questions: as I felt that to complete the inquiry it would be necessary to appoint a new commission to deal with the question, with some very distinguished Mercantile Lawyer at its head

It was always acknowledged in a loose kind of way, and it is stated in every common text-book of Economics, that Credit affects prices in exactly the same way as Gold, and that prices are governed by the aggregate mass of Money and Credit. It was therefore obviously absurd to suppose that the very serious depression which had undoubtedly taken place could be caused solely by a minute falling-off in the supplies of Gold. In order to determine what the effect might be, it was necessary to ascertain as near as might be the ratio of Gold to Credit

The Report of this Commission was felt to be incomplete and unsatisfactory, and in 1886 a new Royal Commission was appointed, with Mr. A. J. Balfour as chairman, to inquire into the causes of the changes in the relative Value of Gold and Silver. After a short time Mr. Balfour's official duties obliged him to resign the chairmanship of the Commission, and Lord Herschell was appointed in his place

Question addressed to the Author by the Commission

2. The Commission did me the honor to request me to lay before them a paper on the relation of Money to Prices. In this paper I explained the broad grounds why Economics can only be made a positive and definite Science by adopting the definition of Wealth as everything whatever which can be bought and sold or exchanged, or whose Value can be measured in money, in accordance with the unanimous doctrine of the ancients for 1300 years ; and that Economics is the Science of Commerce or Exchanges, as it was expressly explained to be by its founders : and that abstract Rights are *Pecunia, Res, Bona,* χρήματα, πράγματα, ἀγαθά, οὐσία : goods, chattels, vendible commodities, merchandise ; as Jurists of all nations have unanimously shown : and modern Economists have acknowledged : that Money and Credit are quantities of exactly the same nature, as a whole line of writers have shown from Aristotle to Mill : and that the system of Credit consists in the Creation, the Sale or Exchange, and the Extinction, of the goods, chattels, commodities or merchandise termed Credits, or Debts

As the exposition of the principles and mechanism of Credit has already been given in the preceding chapters we need not repeat it here

On *the* Ratio *of* Money *to* Credit

3. It is now universally acknowledged that the Circulating Medium, or Currency, or the Measure of Value, in which Prices are expressed, consists of Money and Credit, or Rights to demand Money, in all its forms, written and unwritten. It is therefore evident that we cannot estimate the relation of Money to Prices until we ascertain the ratio of Money to Credit

All Credits payable in Gold—whether Bank Notes, Banking Credits, Bills of Exchange, or any others—have identically the same effects on the Value of Gold and on Prices as an equal quantity of Gold

Similarly, all Credits of whatever form payable in Silver have identically the same effects on the Value of Silver, and prices estimated in silver, as an equal quantity of silver : and the value of gold and silver with respect to each other is determined not only by the actual quantity of the metals themselves, but by the ratio of the aggregate mass of Gold, and all Credits payable in Gold, to the aggregate mass of Silver and all Credits payable in Silver

We may mention an instance well known to the officials of the India Office. The fall in the Value of Silver has been usually attributed to the increased supplies from the mines, and the diminished demand for it, owing to its demonetisation by Germany and various other countries

These circumstances have no doubt had a powerful effect : but there is another which has never, that we have seen, been taken into the popular account

A good many years ago the bills which were drawn by the Council in London on the Indian Governments to meet payments in London due in Gold never exceeded three millions. But of late years these bills have increased to about twenty millions. Now these bills have exactly the same effect on the value of silver as an equal quantity of silver. This increase of about seventeen millions of Council bills have exactly the same effect as an additional supply of seventeen millions from the mines : and just by so much they have increased the embarrassment of the Indian Government

But Credits of all kinds are made payable in specie : hence in every system of Credit there must be an ultimate reserve of specie in order to enable it to maintain its value

From this it is often supposed that there is some definite fixed ratio between Money and Credit : or in mathematical language, that Credit is a function of money

But this is not so : Credit is not a fixed definite function of Money : but it is, if we may coin the term, a contingent function of Money

By which we mean that though in every system of Credit there must be an ultimate reserve of specie, yet that ultimate reserve does not bear a constant fixed ratio to the quantity of Credit ; but it entirely depends on the organisation of Credit : the more highly organised is the system of Credit, the less is the requisite amount of the ultimate reserve of specie

The notion that Money must bear a defined fixed ratio to Credit is founded on the idea of Torrens and Mill, which we shall have to examine at greater length in a future chapter, that all Bills of Exchange, Cheques, &c., are ultimately really paid in Money. Such no doubt was very probably the case 300 years ago : but this was only the very earliest and rudest organisation of Credit

In Chapter III. we have shown that besides payment in Money, there are three other methods by which Obligations are extinguished :—(1) *Acceptilation*, or Release ; (2) *Novation*, or Renewal or Transfer : and (3) *Compensation*, where mutual debts are payments of each other

All ideas that debts are only paid in money are utterly obsolete. In fact, in modern times not one bill in 10,000 is ever paid in money, but by the other three methods described in that chapter

We shall now show that any amount of Credit may be created and used as Money without any relation to the quantity of Money

(1) Before the Continental bankers discounted Bills of Exchange, there used to be great fairs at the principal towns, Lyons, Antwerp, Nuremberg, Hamburg, and many others, held every three months

Continental merchants did not make their bills payable at their own houses, where they would have been obliged to keep a stock of specie to meet them : but they made them payable only at these fairs. In the meantime their bills circulated throughout the country and got covered with indorsements, performing all the functions of money

On a fixed day of the fair the merchants met and exchanged their acceptances with each other : these acceptances reciprocally paid and discharged each other : and the obligations were extinguished by the principle of *Compensation*

By this means Boisguillebert says that obligations to the amount of 80,000,000 were extinguished without the use of a sou in money

(2) When the Bank of England was directed to suspend cash payments in 1797 the Act did not extend to Scotland. But the Scotch banks agreed to refuse all payment of their notes in cash : and this they maintained during the whole course of the war.

And though they were liable to an action for so doing, no action was brought against a Scotch Bank during the whole period. It became the custom to cut the £1 notes in halves and quarters to represent 10s. and 5s. Thus for 20 years the whole commerce of Scotland was carried on without the use of a single guinea

But though the Banks refused payment of their notes to the public, they maintained their system of rigorous exchanges among themselves, so that no single bank was able to continue over-issues : because if it did so it would have had to pay its notes in gold or Bank of England notes to its competitors. In consequence of this the Scotch Bank Notes always maintained an equality in value with Bank of England notes, though of course they shared their depreciation

(3) We have shown that if two persons are customers of the same Bank one of them may pay a debt to the other by giving him a cheque on his account. The creditor may then pay this cheque into his account, and the Credit is transferred from the account of the Debtor to that of the Creditor. This is a *Novation,* which is in all respects equivalent to a payment in money

It is obvious that the larger a bank is, the more numerous are such transactions among its customers : and thus the more payments are made by transfers of Credit, and not by Money : and therefore the larger a Bank is the smaller is the amount of gold required to be held in reserve

(4) But though the persons dealing with each other may not be customers of the same Bank, yet by the system of Clearing, Cheques, Notes, Bills, &c., are transferred just as easily from all the Banks who join in it to each other as Credits are transferred from one customer to another in the same Bank. In the year 1889 Credits to an amount exceeding £7,000,000,000 were interchanged between the Banks in the London Clearing· House alone, without the use of a single coin

And every considerable town in the Kingdom has a Clearing House of its own ; though they do not publish their accounts : and therefore we have no means of ascertaining their amounts

Now let us suppose that all the Clearing Houses in the country were dissolved, and we reverted to the old and barbarous method of paying all debts in actual gold, the amount that would be required would be something enormous : no one can tell what it would be : probably some scores of millions

All these instances prove the doctrine that we stated : that though in every system of Credit there must be an ultimate reserve of gold : yet the ratio of Credit to Gold is not a definite fixed ratio : but that it depends very greatly on the perfection of the organisation of Credit : the more highly organised the system of Credit is, the less is the amount of gold required

When the Bank of Scotland was founded, it was enabled to support £50,000 of its Notes in circulation on a basis of £10,000 in gold: therefore the ratio of Credit to Money was as 5 to 1.

The published accounts of the Joint-Stock Banks in England show that the gold reserve they keep is about 1 to 10 of their liabilities

But in Scotland the system of Credit is still more highly organised and developed than in England, and the last published accounts shew that on a gold reserve of about £4,000,000, they are enabled to support liabilities of about £95,000,000, or the ratio of gold to Credit is about 1 to 23

It has been shown that taking Mercantile and Banking Credit together, the quantity of Credit is to the quantity of Money about 99 to 1

On the Effective Force of Money compared to the Effective Force of Credit

4. The preceding figures show that the absolute quantity of Credit to Money in this country is about 99 to 1. That is to say, that in all prices, 99 parts consist of Credit and only one part of Gold : so that if it were possible to imagine that the whole mass of Credit were annihilated, gold would rise to about 100 times its present value

But even this gives no adequate idea of the Effective Force of Credit as compared to the Effective Force of Money ; because the Effective Force of Money and Credit is measured not only by their absolute amount ; but by their amount multiplied into their velocity of circulation

Now, as a matter of fact, in Scotland the quantity of money in circulation is absolutely infinitesimal. The actual specie lies quiescent in the Banks, merely to inspire confidence in the people that it may be had if required

The whole effective work of the country is done by Bank Notes. While the money lies in the Banks the Notes pass from hand to hand. No one can have the most distant idea as to the number of times that the Bank Notes pass in circulation compared to any minute quantity of money

Reply to the Dogma of Smith, that an Increase of Money can have no effect on the Rate of Interest

5. The expression, Value of Money, being applied to the purchase of two distinct species of merchandise, namely, material commodities, where the Value of Money means the quantity of goods the Money will purchase : and Debts where the Value of Money is measured by the Interest or the Discount, has given rise to some considerations of a somewhat subtle nature, which we must endeavour to unravel

The Rate of Interest or Discount depends on the ratio of the Money to the Debts, just in the same way as the exchangeable relations of Money and commodities are determined

It might therefore at first sight appear that a great increase in the precious metals which leads to a diminution in the Value of Money with respect to one of these classes of merchandise should also necessarily lead to a diminution in the Value of Money with respect to the other

That is to say, if the Value of Money were to diminish so with respect to commodities that it required double the quantity of money to purchase any amount of commodities, that it would follow that the Rate of Interest would fall to one-half. And conversely, that if the Value of Money should fall to one-half in the purchase of Debts, that therefore the quantity of specie necessary to purchase commodities would be doubled. It would appear that such an idea as that the Value of Money could diminish one-half with respect to commodities and remain the same with respect to Debts was paradoxical and untenable

Accordingly, Smith says[1] that several eminent writers had maintained that the increase of the quantity of gold and silver in consequence of the discovery of the South American mines was the real cause of the lowering of the Rate of Interest throughout the greater part of Europe. These metals, they say, having become of less value (*i.e.*, of less purchasing power with respect to commodities) themselves, the use of any particular portion of them became of less value too, and consequently the price which should be paid for it

To this obviously fallacious reasoning, Smith replies—"The following very short and plain argument, however, may serve to explain more distinctly the fallacy which seems to have misled these gentlemen. Before the discovery of the Spanish West Indies, 10 per cent. seems to have been the common rate of interest through the greater part of Europe. It has since that time in different countries sunk to 6, 5, 4, and 3 per cent. Let us suppose that in every particular country the value of silver has sunk precisely in the same proportion, and that in those countries, for example, where interest has been reduced from 10 to 5 per cent. the same quantity of silver can now purchase just half the quantity of goods which it would have purchased before. This supposition will not, I believe, be found anywhere agreeable to the truth, but it is the most favorable to the opinion which we are going to examine, and even upon this supposition it is utterly impossible that the lowering of the Value of silver could have the smallest tendency to lower the rate of interest. If a hundred pounds are in those countries now of no more value than fifty pounds were then, ten pounds must now be of no more value than five pounds were then. Whatever were the causes which lowered the value of the capital, the same must necessarily have lowered that of the interest, and exactly in the same proportion. The proportion between the value of the capital and that of the interest must have remained the same though the rate had never been altered. By altering the rate, on the contrary,

[1] *Wealth of Nations*, Bk. II., ch. iv.

the proportion between these two values is necessarily altered. If a hundred pounds are worth now no more than fifty were then, five pounds can be worth no more than two pounds ten shillings were then. By reducing the rate of interest, therefore, from 10 to 5 per cent., we give for the use of a capital which is supposed to be equal to one-half of its former value, an interest which is equal to one-fourth only of the value of the former interest"

Smith's refutation of the argument alleged for supposing that the increase of money reduced the rate of interest is perfectly conclusive. The fact simply is this : the rate of interest comprehends two elements, one part of the profits paid for the use of the money, the other as insurance for the risk of loss. Now, no diminution in the value of money with respect to commodities can make the slightest difference in respect to these two elements. Whatever the quantity of goods be, more or less, that £100 will purchase, the part of the profits paid for the use of the money will still be the proportion of the £100. Nor can any alteration in the value of money have the slightest effect in influencing the risk of the transaction. Whether the usual price of goods be £100 or £50, it can make no difference in the proportion of the profits agreed to be paid for the use of £100 : nor in the risk : consequently, it can have no influence whatever on the rate of interest

Smith's refutation, then, of the particular argument is perfectly conclusive. Nevertheless his general doctrine, that an increase of money can have no influence on the rate of interest, which has been followed by many other writers, is entirely erroneous, as it is quite easy to show

The sole difficulty in the case is this : Smith and all modern Economists admit that Bank Notes, Bills of Exchange, &c., are circulating Capital, which perform all the functions of money. But they fail to grasp and retain hold of the conception that Rights of Action, such as Credits or Debts, are goods and chattels, commodities or merchandise, just like any material commodities, and that their value is governed by exactly the same laws as that of any other goods

Now, let us suppose that a great and sudden increase of money takes place, as happened in the 16th century ; then it is evident that its effect, on the value of both species of merchandise, Debts and goods, must be exactly identical

If the whole increased quantity of money were applied to the purchase of commodities, that would raise the price of goods

If the whole increased quantity of money were applied to the purchase of mercantile Debts, that would manifestly raise the price of mercantile Debts, *i.e.*, it would lower the rate of interest.

If part of the increased quantity of money were applied to purchase goods and part to purchase Debts, that would raise the price of both, that is, it would raise the price of goods and would lower the rate of interest at the same time

Now, this is what actually happened at the time alluded to. Contemporary writers observed that the price of goods was considerably raised by the influx of money : but only to half the extent which might have been expected.   But they also observed that the average rate of interest was considerably reduced.   And the above reasoning clearly explains these observed historical facts

A greatly increased quantity of Credit has identically the same effects : no more striking instance of which can be imagined than what has taken place in this country

Every one knows that, without going too much into details, an enormous rise has taken place in the price of commodities since the time of William the Conqueror.   This is partly, no doubt, to be accounted for by the depreciation of the Coinage, as there is only about one-third of the amount of metal in the coinage at the present day.   That would account for the nominal prices being tripled : and there has undoubtedly been a very large increase in the amount of specie which would account for another large amount.   But allowing for these causes, there is still an immense residual increase, which can by no possibility be accounted for by these causes

By the Statutes of Eton College, it was enacted that on a certain day in the year all persons on the foundation should receive half a sheep or threepence, the value of half a sheep in 1441.

The Fellows of the College had in recent times interpreted this in their own favor by taking to themselves the value of half a sheep in modern money. But they restricted the gift to the Collegers to a literal threepence. One day, as the Bursar was distributing these threepenny bits to the Collegers at dinner, as was the custom, an audacious young Tug, as Mr. Montague Williams tells us, demanded half a sheep instead: for which temerity he got soundly flogged

Now why has a sheep risen in price from 6d. in 1441 to 50s. or 60s. at the present day?

In the days of Charles II. the usual average rate of interest was 10 per cent. But soon afterwards the institution of bankers and of the Bank of England brought it down to about 3 per cent., at which it has remained to the present day

Now what has been the cause of this very great increase in the price of commodities, and very great fall in the rate of interest?

It is to be found in the amazing increase of Banking Credits in the last two centuries and a-half

The history of Commerce in those days is extremely obscure. But there is no doubt that if the system of discounting Bills of Exchange did not originate with the goldsmith bankers, at least it received a prodigious extension. The greater part of the money of the country having come into their hands, as is described in the next chapter, for which they paid interest, they had to employ it so as to make a profit. This they did by discounting mercantile bills, for which they competed, and so naturally raised their price. But their power of discounting much exceeded the sums placed with them by their customers. Because they did not discount these mercantile bills with cash: but they simply gave their customers a Credit in their books: that is, they issued a Right of action against themselves. They soon found that they could maintain in circulation an amount of Notes several times exceeding the cash they held. In this rude elementary state of Credit, they probably could not maintain in circulation an amount of Notes more than four or five times exceeding the cash they held. But this had all the practical effects of multiplying their cash four or five times

When banking was first started the usual rate of interest was from 8 to 10 per cent., and the bankers allowed their customers 6 per cent. interest on their daily balances payable at demand. But these halcyon days for customers soon passed away. The increased number of bankers multiplied banking Credits faster than the increase of mercantile bills, and by the further foundation of the Bank of England, banking Credits increased so much that the average rate of interest had fallen to 3 per cent. : at which it may be considered to have remained up till the present time

This lowering of the average rate of interest had the effect of immensely raising the value of all property of the form of an Annuity. Thus, when in the reign of Charles II., the average rate of interest was 10 per cent., land was only worth 10 years purchase : but when the average rate of interest was reduced to 3 per cent., the theoretical value of land rose to 33 years purchase

At this time also began that immense rise in the value of all kinds of commodities : as is noticed in the life of Lord Godolphin

Thus, the immense increase of Banking Credits produced exactly the same effects in England in raising the prices of all commodities and lowering the rate of interest, as the great influx of the precious metals did throughout Europe in the 16th century

As far as we have observed, it would appear that the average rate of interest when Money alone was used, before the use of Credit, was from 20 to 25 per cent. : it is the vast increase of Banking Credits which have brought it down to 3 per cent.: and it would almost seem that the average rate in England is likely to be even lower than that

Was the great Depression in Prices from 1873 due to the diminished supplies of Gold?

6. The preceding considerations will enable us to form a judgment on the doctrine which was so stoutly maintained by many persons, that the great depression in the prices of commodities which began in 1873 was entirely due to a slight diminution in the supplies of gold from the mines

Taking the Equation of Value—

$$A = B$$

Let A represent the Circulating Medium, or Currency, which is the Measure of Value, in which Prices are expressed, which consists of Metallic Money and Credit in all its forms, both written and unwritten

Let B represent all other commodities

Then a change in Prices, or the Value of commodities, takes place, either from a change in A : or a change in B : or which is more usual and far more complicated, from a simultaneous change both in A and in B

Now, it is a well-known fact that since 1873 many things have occurred to lower the price of commodities generally, classed under B. Diminished cost of production, increased facilities of transport enabling agricultural products of all sorts to be imported from a wider area, and scientific discoveries, as has been well set forth by Sir Lyon Playfair in several articles, have all tended to lower prices : and all these have had a certain effect. The Report of the Commission attributed much of this to overproduction : nor are we concerned to deny its effect in some cases

But when we consider A, or the Circulating Medium, or the Currency, or the Measure of Value in which Prices are expressed, the report of the Commission is extremely defective. They had no conception of anything beyond a slight diminution in the supplies of gold : and popular opinion attributed the general depression almost exclusively to this cause

Now, the considerations set forth in the preceding chapters show that such an idea is perfectly untenable. It is perfectly acknowledged that Credit produces exactly the same effect on Prices as Gold. And it has been shown by authentic statistics, that in modern times Gold only forms about 1 per cent. of the Circulating Medium, or Currency. And to suppose that a variation to the small extent of a fraction of 1 per cent. on the amount of the Circulating Medium, or the Measure of Value, could produce the effect so popularly attributed to it, is wholly beyond reason

Now, allowing that there were other causes at work to produce this depression, one most potent cause of the depression of prices was wholly overlooked in the Report and in public discussions—namely, the total collapse of speculation after 1873

All speculation is carried on by means of Bills of Exchange. Vast quantities of Bills of Exchange, a large part being of a most illegitimate nature, are created, which partly aggravate the price of commodities, and whose magnitude is partly caused by the expected rise in the prices of commodities, are manufactured. These Bills of Exchange are discounted by Banks, and consequently give rise to an immense increase in Deposits, or Banking Credits : and this vast increase of Credits, both Mercantile and Banking, inflates the Measure of Value, and raises the price of commodities all round

Then, when the bubble bursts, and a great Commercial Crisis ensues, vast amounts of Credit are destroyed : and so the volume of the Measure of Value is diminished, which produces a general lowering of prices all round. It is these vast expansions and contractions of Credit which produce those changes in price which are so ruinous to traders, infinitely more than any minute differences in the quantity of gold

Now, it is well known that 1873 was a period of enormous speculation, and the torrents of Credit created by the speculators raised the price of commodities to an extravagant height. But after 1873 came the collapse : and this speculative Credit being destroyed, prices fell as rapidly as they had risen

As far as this, then, there was nothing extraordinary : or what had not happened times without number before. What was really remarkable and unprecedented, was the long period of the depression

On former occasions great speculations had taken place, giving rise to great rises in price : then the Crisis, which inevitably followed, produced a great depression in prices, and a reduction in the rate of interest

But this fall in prices and in the rate of interest pinched

severely all persons of narrow income, and they cast about for more remunerative investments. Then speculators saw their opportunity: and got up all sorts of fraudulent schemes to entrap the unwary. Thus, speculation bred depression: and depression in its turn bred speculation, in constantly occurring cycles

Now, these alternating cycles of speculation and depression are innate in the system of Credit: and the truth of this is amply proved by the history of commerce in all countries since the vast expansion of the system of Credit, which took place in the latter half of the seventeenth century. And the most important and complicated problems in Economics is to know how to deal with these Commercial Crises when they arise: to bring them under scientific control: and to prevent them from developing into Monetary Panics: which are the most fearful calamities of modern times

Now, one of the principal causes of the great depression since 1873 is, that speculation on a large scale has, from whatever cause, been totally extinct. Either men have learnt wisdom from experience, or they have been unable to discover any commodities to speculate in: or they have been unable to discover schemes to entrap the unwary. It is not the depression itself, but its unprecedented length, which is in any way remarkable: and, in fact, it requires no further observations

The preceding considerations show how utterly insoluble it is to ascertain the precise influence of a little more, or a little less, gold on prices. It is infinitely more complicated than the influx of the precious metals in the sixteenth century

At that time there was scarcely a Bank in Europe, except in Italy: and when an increase of gold took place, it came at once into contact with commodities, and, therefore, inevitably raised their price

But in modern times an increased quantity of gold is first of all paid into Banks, and thus forms a basis for them to enlarge their Credits, and so reduce the rate of interest: and the comparatively minute quantities of gold are buried amid such a stupendous mass of Banking Credits, that the most subtle analysis in the world is wholly incompetent to separate the effects of Gold from those of Credit. It is infinitely more easy to estimate the effects of Gold and Credit combined, than those of Gold alone

One thing may be safely said, many persons are in alarm that the increased use of gold as the standard money by various nations may lead to a permanent enhancement of its value, and a depression of prices. Such fears are wholly futile: the earth teems with gold: and even if it were not so, our present system of Credit is capable of a still higher simplification and organization than at present exists: and by such improvement, a given amount of gold might be made to support a much larger amount of Credit than it actually does

A. P. BLUNDELL, TAYLOR & CO.. PRINTERS, &C., 177, UPPER THAMES STREET, LONDON.